How to Speak Alien

Invading Your Teens' World Without Invading Their Space

Michael Ross

Beacon Hill Press of Kansas City
Kansas City, Missouri

Copyright 2001
by Beacon Hill Press of Kansas City

ISBN 083-411-8815

Printed in the
United States of America

Cover Design: Michael Walsh
Cover Illustration: Keith Alexander

Library of Congress Cataloguing-in-Publication Data

Ross, Michael, 1961-
    How to speak alien : invading your teens' world without invading their space / Michael
    Ross.
    p. cm.
    ISBN 0-8341-1881-5 (pb.)
    1. Parent and teenager. 2. Parent and teenager—Religious aspects—Christianity. 3. Parenting. 4. Adolescent psychology. 5. Teenagers—Religious life. I. Title.
    HQ799.15.R674 2001
    306.874—dc21

                                                                        00-069759

10   9   8   7   6   5   4   3

To my mother, Ruth. You raised six of us all by yourself,
and you did it well.
To Floyd and Bonnie Cox, the parents of my wife, Tiffany.

CONTENTS

INTRODUCTION
A World of Extremes

"Don't look down!" the 13-year-old tells herself over and over. "Stay focused on the goal—just as Dad showed me. I won't get stuck. I won't fall. I can do this."

The teen reaches above her head and grips a tiny crevice with her fingertips and slowly inches up the steep rock face—inch by inch.

"Go, Spiderwoman!" her dad cheers from above.

"You're climbing like a pro, honey," her mom shouts.

The encouragement feels good. It gives the girl courage and keeps her going as she attempts her first parent/teen rock climbing adventure.

Suddenly, panic. "Uh . . . I need help, Mom—Dad," the girl yells. "There's no place to go. I'm stuck."

She has reached a point on the wall that's smooth and slippery. Adrenaline surges through the girl's veins and every muscle seems to tremble.

"Think it through," her father says calmly. "Remember what I taught you. Stay focused, take your time, and look for handholds."

The girl spots one and grips it with her fingertips and pushes with her legs. Then she notices another . . . and another one after that. Before she realizes it, triumph! She joins her parents at the top.

Her mom and dad give her bear hugs. The girl soaks in the view—and the praise. She feels pretty confident standing atop the canyon wall. The panorama from up here looks completely foreign, like standing on the planet Mars. Rugged sedimentary rock fills her view. She deeply breathes the fresh air and the feeling of conquest.

Next challenge: life as a teenager!

This scene is played out repeatedly in the rugged canyons of Moab, Utah, a half-day's drive from my home in Colorado Springs. Each summer, adults and teens invade this remote part of the Southwest to face their fears on a rock face and to build the confidence everyone needs to persevere under pressure. The victories savored in Moab often last a lifetime.

In a similar manner, parenting teenagers involves guiding them up a steep rock face—a rock face known as adolescence. The key to their success depends upon the training they receive from you. Are you instilling confidence in your children? Are you giving them the skills they need to launch boldly into adulthood?

Trained to Win

Face it, the world of teens is a lot like the extreme wilderness of the desert Southwest. Their bodies are going through drastic physical changes. Hormones surge through their veins. Society bombards them with messages that contradict God's standards. The pressures they face cause them to react in ways they've never behaved before, leaving parents to wonder if their precious children have been replaced by evil alien impostors.

Though that last sentence may be a bit excessive, there's no doubt that the world our young people live in is warring for their souls. That's why it's vital that you act on the Proverbs 22:6 promise and train your teen to survive, thrive, and grow in these extreme times. Build in them the . . .

DESIRE to take a stand for what's right in a world that often applauds what's wrong.

COURAGE to be a follower of Christ and to stand on their beliefs even when the easier path would be to give in to worldly pressures.

FAITH to lay down their lives for the cause of Christ.

Train your teen to live according to your *actions,* not just your *words.* The parents in the story taught their daughter to scale the face of the rock by climbing it first. They trained their teen by *what* they did and *how* they did it.

Likewise, if you want your child to follow Christ, you must first be a disciple of Jesus. If you want him or her to read the Bible, you must read it and live by it. Your teen doesn't always hear your words, but he or she certainly sees your actions. Lead by example. Train your teen to "scale" adolescence with confidence.

In the following pages, I'll arm you with some ideas to help you do just that. My goal is to help you relate to your teen by revealing what's going on in an adolescent's head.

The purpose of this book is to show how a teen's world looks and feels. This book examines the keys to building a stronger, positive, lasting relationship between you and your teen. In each chapter you will find a balance of solid advice, bulleted information, and personal stories. I pray this will be an invaluable resource for parents, ministers, and anyone else who works with and loves teens.

Mysteries of the Teen Zone

Riiinnnggg.

Amber hustles into Mrs. LaMotte's first period English class seconds before the door shuts. She grins at a friend and takes her seat in the last desk of the last row. On the outside Amber looks like a typical teen. But the inside is another story.

I feel like I'm in a dark, cold prison cell, she writes in her journal during class. *It's really scary because the walls are closing in and there's no way out. What's the use of going on? Mom and Dad fight all the time . . . they'll probably split up. Grandma's really sick and may die. I hate my brother. I even hate myself. Everything's falling apart and I feel so lonely.*

Amber scribbles one last line in her journal: *If this is living, I don't want to live anymore.*

Jason yanks Brock's Big Mac from his hand and takes a bite. "Go on, Banana Brain . . . ask her," he mumbles, then opens his mouth and exposes the contents.

"Gross!"

Wham! Eric slams his algebra book on Brock's fries and scrapes the remains into a nearby trash can. *"That's* what I call gross," he grins.

"You're history," Brock snaps. "I'm gonna rip your lungs through your armpits and knock your . . ."

The three freeze as a flock of freshman goddesses stream by.

"Cool it!" Eric insists. "Major babe city."

Jason falls on his knees before Brock and goes into his Porky Pig routine. "P-p-p-p-lease, Brocksters, you just g-g-g-otta help us!"

"Not even," Brock answers. "I'm not goin' anywhere near those girls with you rejects around!"

"But they talk to you."

"And with your help, they might talk to us," Eric adds.

"You just killed my lunch! Why should I help?"

"I'll pay you," Jason begs.

Brock's eyes light up. A grin forms on his lips. He flicks a French fry off of Eric's book. "Deal!"

What's with These Teens Today?

What's with kids? What makes them tick? How are they different from kids in my time? What things do they deal with?

I hear these questions a lot, usually from parents. And my answer is always the same. The core issues adolescents deal with today are not much different from those teens have dealt with in the past:

- ❀ Teens live in a world that is playful and childlike one moment, then suddenly changes to harsh, overwhelming, and cruel.
- ❀ Popularity is measured by success with the opposite sex.
- ❀ Rejection is a fate worse than death.
- ❀ Guys' drive for independence is as strong as their drive for food.
- ❀ Girls' drive for independence is as strong as their drive to seemingly live on the phone.
- ❀ They are fascinated by those strange creatures known as "the opposite sex."
- ❀ Their desire for loud, thumping music and their taste in wild haircuts transforms parents into raging, foaming-at-the-mouth maniacs.
- ❀ They can become explosive if family members hug them in public, especially in front of their peers.

This sounds a lot like teens of the past, right? But while young people today may be similar to teens of the past, what has changed for youth today is the world around them. Today's teens face a staggering level of social stresses ranging from increased competition in schools and for jobs to pervasive violence.

Computer technology has exploded, making it much easier for guys and girls to interface with others their own age anywhere in the world through the telecommunication superhighway. And in this day and age of high-tech toys and low-tech values, sin is packaged, downloaded and made accessible to the masses—even the teen masses—as never before.

Let's learn more about the Christian teen. I asked a few young people from across North America to describe their world and what they deal with as a modern teen. Take a look at what they had to say.

⚲ TEEN INSIGHTS ⚲

Chad, 17: Anyone who stands up for anything right these days gets dumped on—me included. I've learned one thing: Christianity won't make you popular at school. I get teased a lot for standing up for what's right.

Kris, 16: I'm into computers, and it's amazing how much temptation you can stumble upon through the Internet. And it seems to be getting easier to access porn and other kinds of garbage with a computer and a modem.

Andy, 16: It hurts to see trusted Christians blowing it, becoming too worldly or falling away altogether. It seems like today's Christian teens are moving to extremes: some are becoming fired up for Christ, while others are becoming wimpy.

Melissa, 15: I sometimes get the feeling that I'm the only virgin my age. Many of my friends, even Christians, brag about how far they went sexually. But I'm committed to staying pure. It often makes me very unpopular.

Brian, 14: I often feel like a lone Christian at school. Lately, I've found myself having to defend my faith to other students, as well as teachers. The public school is a battleground. Students push all kinds of crazy stuff on my campus—everything from drug use to New Age.

Topsy-Turvy World

As a youth worker, I've logged hundreds of hours with teens at amusement parks. On one particular trip I was determined to walk in their shoes, learning as much as I could about their world. I never imagined that a 90-second ride on a roller coaster would give me just about all the insight I needed. Take a look. . . .

◉ ⟆ ⟆ ⟆

I squeezed my eyes shut and gripped the safety bar. "Eeeeeyyoooweeee!"

Seconds after takeoff, the Zambezi Zinger launched into "whiplash mode," blasting around treacherous twists and turns and stretching my face into a dozen different contortions. A bunch of catastrophic possibilities raced through my mind: *We're goin' too fast. We're not gonna make the next curve. We're history!*

Suddenly, the roller coaster slowed and then began a steep, spiral ascent. I took a deep breath and glanced at Marty, a young man I was hanging out with.

"Awesome coaster, isn't it?" he said, giving me a quick high five.

I flashed a forced grin. "Sorry, but my stomach doesn't agree."

"Hey, we're just getting started," Marty said. "There's a lot more ahead. This is sort of the calm before the storm—so hold on."

Calm before the storm? More ahead?

Once at the top, the roller coaster jerked to a stop. I glanced over the edge. For half a millisecond the park looked peaceful. But then the mean machine began its bone-jarring plunge . . . and the world distorted.

"Uh-oh," I mumbled. "This time, there's NO WAY we're gonna make it. This time, we're . . . eeeeeyyoooweeee!"

◉ ⟆ ⟆ ⟆

Loop, lunge, plunge, zip, flip, whirl—these words best describe the sometimes peaceful, mostly topsy-turvy world of teenagers!

Just when your son or daughter feels as if he or she is on top of the world, just when everything seems to be cruising along perfectly . . . emotions plunge and life gets scary.

Adolescence is a roller coaster ride to adulthood. On one

hand, teenagers want to feel independent and grown up. Yet, even though they often don't admit it, they are frightened by the reality of becoming adults. Growing up means leaving home, the very place where they receive so much security and self-esteem. As Larry Dumont, M.D., points out in his book *Surviving Adolescence,* "Since teenagers have not yet felt the self-confidence that comes from independent experience, they are constantly being pushed and pulled between wanting to spread their wings and wanting to stay in the comfortable nest."[1]

Let's move in closer and look at a few primary characteristics of their roller-coaster world.

Peers Gain Influence

The roller coaster ride begins in junior high. As young teens give up their emotional dependence on their parents, they begin to see their parents as ordinary people with strengths and weaknesses instead of the all-wise, all-powerful figures these adults had always seemed to be. As parental power wanes, peer power grows.

Teenage friendship becomes an outgrowth of that struggle between independence and dependence. Suddenly, instead of looking just to their parents for self-esteem, young people begin looking elsewhere—usually to their friends. The love and confidence they used to get primarily from Mom and Dad now comes from peers as well.

Cliques form as young people sort themselves out on the basis of their shared interests. Within a clique, adolescents tend to have similar attitudes toward school, perhaps because schoolwork often impinges on social activities. Unless members have similar values, conflicts may arise over whether to study or party. With their own language, dress code, rules, and similar attitudes toward just about everything, members of a clique form a counterculture—a solid front from which to hide, at least on the surface, their inner uncertainty. Rejection and acceptance become a daily way of life.

Whether the clique is made up of jocks, brains, nerds, burnouts, or social butterflies, both boys and girls get deeply involved in their groups during adolescence. As youngsters pass into middle adolescence and dating becomes important, a particular group of girls begin to hang out with a particular group of boys and a mixed group forms. Each member establishes a close relationship with a member of the other sex, allowing group members to learn about heterosexual relationships within the protection of the clique. By the time they're about 17, membership in the clique has lost some importance and teenagers may find more satisfaction from individual relationships with friends of either sex.

Here are a few quick highlights of the social world of teenagers:

◉ Communicating with their friends on the telephone or by E-mail often becomes a priority in teenagers' lives.

◉ When intimacy involves the disclosure of your innermost feelings, as it does in adolescence, parents no longer seem appropriate confidants.

◉ Girls' friendships are often deeper and more intense than those of boys.

◉ Because of the less intimate nature of boys' friendships, many guys turn to the girls they know when they need to share their secrets and private feelings.

Parents Still Rule

Despite the shift toward peers for acceptance, millennial teens still believe that parents exert the greatest influence over their lives.

A report from Barna Research Group, Ltd., "Third Millennium Teens,"[2] indicates that out of 1,028 junior highers and high school students, 84.5 percent believe that parents do best at delivering love and safety. In other words, most teens still look to their moms and dads for guidance. The Barna survey concludes that parents provide what young people need to maximize personal potential, to feel positive about themselves, and to handle the challenges of life.

Sean, 18, of Los Angeles agrees: "My friends are important to me, but they'll never replace my parents. Consistently throughout my life, Mom and Dad told me that they loved me and that they were always there for me. Those messages really stuck with me—especially when my friends pressured me to do stuff that was wrong.

"Instead of getting myself into a stupid situation, I'd go to my parents for advice. I trust what they say and know that they'll help me make good decisions."

Everything Is in a Constant State of Change

How teenagers respond to their changing bodies depends on the reactions of family and friends, on their own personalities, and on whether or not their bodies meet cultural standards of attractiveness. If youngsters know what to expect, and if their parents have made them feel comfortable about changes in the way they look and feel, they will take puberty in stride. If they enter puberty with high self-esteem, they're more likely to wind up pleased than embarrassed when their growing is done.

Here's a tremendous way you can help your teen: try walking in his or her shoes. Take a moment to consider what life was like for you as a teenager. What aspect of your physical development was most embarrassing? How did you feel about it? Do you think your parents knew what was bothering you? Did they ever discuss it with you? Now think about what involvement you would have liked your parents to have had.

Above all, be sensitive to the changes going on in your teen's life. Never make fun of physical developments such as height and weight. According to psychologist Bruce Narramore, "Some parents attempt to motivate their children through sarcasm or ridicule. They believe teasing or pressuring teens about excess weight or untidiness will force positive changes. But these pressure tactics only create resentment and strong resistance."[3]

One last thing: do your best to reduce the importance teens place on their bodies as the source of self-esteem. Our culture pays too much attention to people's physical appearance and not enough to other important skills and talents.

Teens Focus on the Moment— Not the Big Picture

A sense of invulnerability—the feeling that "it won't happen to me"—peaks during early adolescence. Before that confidence wanes, many young people have made decisions that affect the rest of their lives. They do so without much experience of the world, using immature cognitive powers and without understanding the consequences of their decisions. Most young adolescents who become sexually active, for example, do not realize that consequences of becoming a teenage parent include losing the world of opportunities that education brings.

Living in a world characterized by instant results adds to the problem. "Today's social pressures place adult demands on teenagers without giving them adequate tools to respond with," points out psychologist David Elkind, "tools such as tested values and examined experience."[4]

Elkind explains that teens often don't have an ethical framework or the experience necessary for coping with adult stress. When that lack is coupled with the false sense of invulnerability, more and more teens turn to self-destructive methods of coping: drug and alcohol abuse, crime, psychological withdrawal, and even suicide.

◎   ☙   ⚶   ৎ

Help your son or daughter sail successfully through the roller coaster teen years. Be available and reassuring. Prepare yourself to provide accurate information and clear values that will help them make sense of their topsy-turvy worlds. And when it comes to the seemingly constant disappointments they face, tell them this:

"As Christians, we know who's in control of this big roller coaster ride of life: Jesus Christ. Our Lord doesn't stay back at the station. He goes with us on the ride—always taking care of us no matter what's around the next turn. And while we don't know what lies ahead of us, we can trust and hope in God. He is molding you into the kind of men and women He wants you to be."

LESSON FROM THE TRENCHES

Living for the Moment

Lissa Halls Johnson, a coworker, told me a story about a young man named Drew. Drew had never thought seriously about life or the consequences of his actions. He was too busy living for the moment. The result: shattered dreams, regrets . . . and a life now filled with misery. Sadly, Drew's attitude epitomizes that of too many teenagers today.

I've reprinted Lissa's story. While this may seem like an extreme example, it should provide more insight into the "sense of invulnerability."[5]

· As I hung up my phone, I put my head on my desk and sobbed. The caller didn't have details. He told me only that Drew had rolled his van the night before and would probably be dead sometime in the next 24 hours.

Drew was one of my best buddies. He lived next door to me on the shores of a lake in northern California. He looked to me as a little sister, and I looked to him as a protective brother. We spent hours with his friends, talked about life, and spent an awful lot of time laughing. They were into parties. I wasn't. Youth made them feel invincible. To them, life was always going to be carefree, easy, and fun. Eternal concerns had no meaning.

Once, Drew and I hiked through a big patch of dried weeds and sat on a huge rock underneath a gnarled oak tree. The summer sun glinted off Drew's blond hair. His laughter echoed off the hills. For the first time, we talked seriously about God, Jesus, and salvation.

"I know God's going to wake me up someday," he told me. "But right now, I'm having too much fun. I've got plenty of time to think about that."

I begged him not to drive after having his "fun."

He shrugged his shoulders like it was no big deal. "I'll probably have an accident someday."

Crash and Coma

Drew and his friends had refined partying to an art. I wasn't invited to the full-fledged parties. It was just as well because I hated being around obnoxious drunks.

The day before Good Friday, a party started in the afternoon. Shortly before midnight, Drew and a friend decided to take a spin in Drew's van. No one knows how fast they were going. But it didn't really matter. A slight curve in the road had been poorly engineered, causing even moderately speeding vehicles to become temporarily airborne. And Drew's mind, hazy from the beer and marijuana, had forgotten this important fact.

As the van catapulted through the air, it spit Drew out, tossing him into a metal signpost, a world of pain . . . and then silence. Drew's head broke a pipe in two, and his right leg tore through his hip socket. Underneath the broken ribs, a lung collapsed; his diaphragm and liver were torn by the impact.

The sound of crunching metal split the night, waking an ambulance driver who lived a block away. Jumping out of bed, he radioed other attendants, and then raced to help.

Drew's heart stopped twice on the long ride over the mountains to the closest hospital with facilities able to care for him.

His parents arrived from Southern California early the next morning, just as Drew was wheeled into intensive care following surgery. Shortly after that, I received the phone call.

Everyone prayed—even Drew's friends who never thought about God. My heart ached with prayers. I got through the day, not really knowing what I'd done.

Drew lived, but he didn't wake up.

They transferred him to a specialty hospital 500 miles away. Three months after the accident, I visited him. I knew he was in a coma, but I wanted to touch him, talk to him, and tell him that I cared about him. I assumed he would look like a peacefully sleeping person. What I saw instead took my breath away. I battled the urge to fall apart.

Drew had changed from an athletic, active, muscular young man to a shriveled, pale rag doll. Dressed only in a loose diaper, he stared at me with no recognition, his eyes eerily following me as I moved about the bed, talking with his parents. It was difficult to understand that the brain can go to sleep, yet the eyes can be open. I tried unsuccessfully to be cheerful. Sitting on the edge of the bed, I searched for things to say but could think of nothing. I couldn't tell him everything would be all right. It was obvious nothing in Drew's world would ever again be all right.

Before I left, his parents told him to kiss me. After the trembling kiss, a grin twisted his mouth . . . he looked like a kid who figured he had gotten away with something. His mother started crying.

"It's his first smile," she said. "You must be very important to him."

But really, I was one of his few visitors. Only one of his other friends *ever* cared to visit.

Like an Old Man

A few weeks later, Drew came out of the coma he'd been in for 16 weeks. We hoped that would make a difference. But it didn't. It was as if he'd been recently born. Six-month-old babies don't walk, feed themselves, go to work or talk. And Drew didn't either. Specialists said he might never progress beyond that mental age.

Drew then spent months in hospitals and rehabilitation centers. Determined therapists, parents, and even infantile Drew refused to accept the devastating verdict. My buddy responded to the encouragement and therapy, but the progress was painfully slow—physically and emotionally. His parents lived in the hospitals with him for 14 months.

When he was eventually released and returned home, Drew relied on his parents for everything. They even had to translate for him when people couldn't understand his garbled speech.

Today, like an old man, Drew shuffles around his apartment. It takes him 10 minutes to go from a vehicle to the front door, 5 minutes to reach the bathroom, and 30 minutes to walk one block to the store. His dream of doing something grand with his life has been reduced to watering indoor plants for local businesses.

Like most humans, Drew longs to share life with someone special. But no one really wants to take the time to understand his slow, guttural speech. No one is patient enough to take a walk with him. His partying friends don't want to see him anymore. They're interested in parties, not in tragic reminders of what such a life can do. So Drew's relationships come through television, magazines, and occasional letters.

Drew now strongly believes in God. He doesn't blame God for his own actions. Instead, his faith gives him a purpose for living.

Sometimes I still think of Drew and cry. I remember the day he shrugged his shoulders when I begged him not to drive after a party.

"I'll probably be in an accident someday," Drew had told me. He truly didn't think it would be any big deal.

Making Contact:
Getting Through to Your Teen

Do you sometimes catch yourself wondering if . . .

- ❧ a computer program inside your teen's head turns ordinary conversations into heated arguments?
- ❧ your 14-year-old son is actually a mutant Neanderthal kid who escaped from the circus?
- ❧ your 16-year-old daughter spends all that time in the bathroom perfecting her plot for world domination?
- ❧ *Webster's* goofed up and the true definition of the word *home* is actually "loony bin; an insane asylum; madhouse"?
- ❧ your teenager has been abducted by aliens and been reprogrammed to create anarchy and to usher in the destruction of society?

If you've ever thought these things, join the crowd. Life as a parent of teenagers can feel more like a *life sentence*—with *no* time off for good behavior. At least, that's the description thousands of weary moms and dads have expressed. That's why this chapter is filled with vital communication strategies: how to really be heard by your teen; the dos and don'ts of making contact; how to reduce the tension level on the home front; and how to know what your teenager thinks and feels instead of having to guess at what's bothering him or her.

So grab a cup of coffee, find a comfortable chair, and let's look at some ways of getting through to your teen.

Communication Meltdown

Imagine if your teenagers freely opened up and shared what's really going on inside their heads. (You'd probably pass out, right?)

And if your son or daughter came home from school speaking in complete sentences—instead of the usual grunts of "Uh-huh," "Naaaa," "I dunno." You'd be making a frantic 911 call: "I'd like to report impostors on the premises. They say they're my kids, but I know better!"

It's a strange teenage quirk. Sometime on or before his or her 13th birthday, the average kid transforms from an enthusiastic, wide-eyed elementary child to an emotionally unpredictable, uncommunicative alien.

But let me give you a word of encouragement. During my 15 years of experience with teenagers, I've observed that just beneath the alien exteriors are enthusiastic, wide-eyed teens who have heads full of hopes, dreams, fears, and questions. With a little prompting, they're very capable of sharing what's going on inside their minds—especially with Mom and Dad.

And while I know it is often hard to communicate with your teen, I urge you to try. You are the greatest influence in your teen's life. And even though he or she doesn't always show it, your teen's heart is tuned to the "parent frequency." Make it a priority to invade your teen's world daily and to foster meaningful communication. (More than just "Uh-huh" and "I dunno.")

Right now you might be thinking, *I'd love to get my kids talking, Mike, but how? I try to carry on a simple conversation, and they shut down. I make an effort to give my advice . . . and it doesn't get through. But our youth minister, and just about any other trusted adult, can merely clear their throats and they're all ears. What gives?*

What gives is the "War of Independence," that constant, tension-filled struggle parents everywhere experience as their teens rocket toward adulthood. But in the preceding paragraph we touched upon an essential teenage need—a key that can unlock the door to your child's world; a key that can help you over the barriers to solid conversation.

This communication link is called *trust*. It's fragile and sometimes hard to build, but it's universally important. It's also a primary reason why your youth minister—and just about any other *trusted* adult—can command your teen's full attention.

Let's take a look at three ways trust can spark conversation:

Communication Key 1

Trust earns you the right to be heard. Isn't "your right" already guaranteed simply because you're a parent? It should be, but in the real world it isn't. Your teens are focused on the here and now. They're probably not thinking about all the sacrifices you've made for them through the years or even how much you love them. But they will, almost instantaneously, recall the "injustices" you've caused: your "countless" broken promises, the times you blamed them for things they insisted they didn't do, days when you were "too busy." While perfect parenthood should never be your goal, it is important to build trust by earning the right to be heard. How? It starts with the next two steps.

Communication Key 2

Your attention builds trust. Teens know that love shown by parents says, "Your life is important, daughter [or son], and I'm going to give you my time." Spend time with them, show them you will listen and talk and work things out together. Invade their world . . . and let them invade yours.

Communication Key 3

Breathing room = trust. Invading their world should be balanced with plenty of space. Invading their world doesn't mean you continually nose into their business. Teens need room to grow, to make their own decisions. This is crucial for their development into responsible adults.

Communication Basics

Most of us understand as much about communication as we do about the inner workings of our TVs, so we don't know very much. When it comes to watching the tube, we simply plop down on the couch, punch the remote, and are instantly informed and entertained. We laugh and cry at the messages beamed at us, without considering how picture and sound signals are transmitted to our television or how electrons are bombarding the back of our screen. That is, until the TV breaks down—leaving us staring at a blank screen.

Like many parents, you probably feel the same way about talking with your teen. You press the power button on your "conversation remote," tune in a topic, and if you're really interested, turn up the volume. But when static is in your teen's reception—when communication shuts down altogether or when you discover you're not speaking the same language—you suddenly feel as if you're staring at a blank screen. What should you do? (After all, your teen didn't come with an owner's manual.)

Exactly why is it so hard to get through to your teen sometimes?

The difficulty may stem from the same reasons your teen has a hard time getting through to you. One of the most common complaints I hear from teens is that even though they want to communicate with their parents, they are turned off by *what* their parents say and *how* they say it.

Case in Point . . .

I'm convinced that somewhere there is a list of "sacred parent sayings" that each generation of parents is expected to pass down to their kids. Here's a selection of these sayings. As you read these sayings, count the ones you have used this week on your kids (as well as the ones your parents used on you):

- ◎ "As long as you're living under this roof, you'll do exactly as I say. End of discussion!"
- ◎ "You're *not* going anywhere until your room is clean."
- ◎ "This is going to hurt me far more than it's going to hurt you."
- ◎ "If only you acted more like your sister."
- ◎ "It's not that I don't trust you; it's just that I don't trust your choice of friends."
- ◎ "Someday, when you're older, you'll understand."
- ◎ "Clean your room—it looks like a pigsty. Were you born in a barn?"
- ◎ "I don't like your attitude. Do you want to be grounded for life?"
- ◎ "Do I look like I'm made out of money?"
- ◎ "Would you jump off a bridge if everyone else did it?"
- ◎ "In my day, we didn't let our rooms get this filthy."

☿ TEEN INSIGHTS ☿

What do you wish your parents would understand about you?

Tracy, 17, Colorado Springs: I wish they'd realize that I'm not a bad kid and that I really try hard at everything I do. They're overprotective and too afraid that I'm going to mess up my life. I will fall on my face and make mistakes on occasion. That's how I learn.

Jerry, 16, Harrisonburg, Virginia: I hate it when Mom and Dad talk down to me, as if I'm still a little kid. I'm growing up and becoming a man. Soon I'll be responsible for my own life. As much as they'd love to change that, they just can't. That's the way it is.

Shacristala, 18, Pasadena, California: I need their attention. But all my father is concerned about is work and reading the paper. He never talks to me or to my mom. He never comes to my plays or concerts. He has no interest in my life. It's like he doesn't even care about me.

How do you feel about your family's rules?

Kris, 17, Indianapolis: When I want to go out with my friends and my parents say no, I try to back down and listen to what they have to say. But at times it's worth arguing. Even if you don't get to go, they get to see your viewpoint.

Lance, 16, Houston: I realize that a family couldn't function without rules, but my parents are too rigid at times. I wish they'd lighten up and stop lecturing me about stuff. Getting on my case about every little thing only makes me angry inside— and closes the doors to communication.

What should parents expect of their kids?

Jon, 16, Indianapolis: My parents expect me to do really well in school. When I don't, they're disappointed, and they give me a hard time about it. Sometimes I just need another chance. So we agreed that when I prove myself, they'll stop pestering me.

Chrissy, 15, Oklahoma City: It's hard for me to go to my parents with a problem, because I don't want them to think bad of me. If they want me to open up more, then don't expect me to be perfect.

Keys to Making Contact

Communication with your teen is a two-way street. Effective communication requires input from both parties. You already know most teens are reluctant to take the first steps to get it started—so beginning communication is up to you. Since you're reading this book, you probably want to move beyond the list of "sacred parent sayings." The key to a good relationship lies in caring communication that is committed, empathetic, and clear. This can significantly reduce friction on the home front by offering solid direction.

"Like wet clay, teens are still malleable," says pastor Paul W. Swets in his book *The Art of Talking with Your Teenager.* "They are breaking out of their childhood molds and entering a new and qualitatively different realm of thinking, feeling and acting. It is confusing but exciting. Teenagers need their parents' knowledge and support to survive."[1]

Learning to "speak alien" and truly connecting with teens begins by putting yourself in their shoes. Do you remember the embarrassment, the awkward moments, the times of hilarity as well as agony you experienced as a teenager? Try to consider the changes they're enduring. You'll understand your teenager better if you can remember your own phases of adolescent development.

Next, try these six keys to making contact. They'll help you open doors to mutual respect and understanding. And that's what "learning to speak alien" is all about!

Key 1: Watch What You Say and *How* You Say It

The best intentions in the world can backfire if you use the wrong words. Phrases like "You never," "You always," "You don't ever" sound accusing and can cause your teen to become defensive and ultimately to shut down. When you speak, stress your particular wants and feelings by using "I." For example, saying, "I want" or "I feel" are effective places to begin.

Don't pile on a bunch of criticisms when you talk. Stick to the original topic of discussion. Pulling up unrelated and unresolved hurt feelings from the past and introducing them into a new conflict only confuses matters and isn't fair. It sends a message to your teen that you're keeping score on everything he or she does do wrong. It immediately puts your child on the defensive.

Look at the scenario below. Do you understand how Conversation 2 is more effective to get through to your teen?

Daughter: Mom, do you know where I put my glasses?

Conversation 1
Mother: How many times do I have to tell you to keep track of your things and learn to put them away—especially an expensive pair of glasses?
Daughter: I didn't ask for a lecture, Mom. I asked for your help. Besides, you lose stuff all the time.

Conversation 2
Mother: I believe you left them on the dining room table.
Daughter: Thanks, Mom.

According to Robert S. McGee author and founder of Rapha, a national organization that provides family counseling services, our home environment plays a central role in forming our beliefs and emotions. "Parents," he says, "have a powerful impact on a child's outlook and behavior." In his book *The Search for Significance,* McGee gives an example of how one parent's constant negative communication shattered a teenager's self-esteem:

Scott grew up in a home without praise, discouraged by his parents whenever he attempted anything new and challenging. After years of hearing, "You'll never be able to do anything, Scott, so don't even try," he began to believe it himself. Neither Scott nor his parents could later understand why he had flunked out of college and was continually shuffling from one job to another, never able to achieve success. Believing he was doing the best he could do, but suspecting he would always fail, Scott constantly performed according to his false self-perception.[2]

Key 2: Take Interest in What Your Teen Has to Say

A few years back, a TV talk show on parent-teen relations confirmed the need for parents to take a stronger interest in their kids. Teen after teen shared stories of heartache about life at home with parents who were out of touch with their kids. As the show ended, the host asked the audience for their comments. A 14-year-old boy stood with his mother and shared these words with a national TV audience: "This is my mom. She knows me."

You can close the gap by taking a genuine interest in your teen and his or her world. Tune into feelings and try to look at events at home or at school from your teen's point of view, as well as your own. If your teen senses that you don't really understand or care, he or she will stop listening to you. But when you're clearly doing your best to understand, the chances are much greater that your teen will tune into you.

Despite how it feels at times, teenagers really do want their parents to talk to them; they want to believe they have someone who will listen, who will understand, who will make them feel better. Just ask the boy who affirmed his mom on national TV.

Key 3: Learn to Listen

One of the biggest complaints I've heard from teenagers is that their parents just don't listen. "My parents don't understand me." "We can't seem to communicate." "Things could be better if they'd just give me a chance—and listen!"

Listening is where effective communication really begins. In fact, the best communication tool God gave us is not our lips, but our ears.

One dad strengthened his relationship with his teenage daughter just by taking the time to ask a simple, caring question—then listening to his child's response. Here's what happened.

At a morning church service, the pastor preached about how important it is for fathers to spend time with their children. The minister explained that fathers need to spend time alone with each child every day, suggesting that they go for a walk, or out to dinner or just stay home and play a game.

After the service, the dad took his daughter aside and told her how badly he wanted to be that kind of father. Then he explained how guilty he felt after hearing the message, and asked how she felt. The girl opened up.

"You haven't done any of the things the pastor mentioned since I was a little girl," she explained. "At times I feel neglected. All you do is work, and that makes me wonder if you really love me. I want us to spend more time together. It would mean a lot to me."

Most teens want to communicate with their parents, but they just don't know where to begin. If you will ask the right questions—then listen to their answers—you'll give them a place to start.

Dr. Thomas Gordon, in his book *Parental Effectiveness Training (P.E.T.) in Action,* identifies four skills of effective listening:[3]

- ◉ **Passive listening (or silence).** Give your teen a chance to speak.

- ◉ **Acknowledgment responses.** Don't just stand with a blank expression on your face. Even when you're listening passively, it's a good idea to make sincere comments, such as "I see" or "Oh?" emphasizing that you are paying attention.

- ◉ **Door openers.** These are simple, nonjudgmental statements, such as "I was wondering how you feel about having a family night out, instead of going out with your friends?" These simple invitations may feel awkward—or may feel as if you're giving away your parental authority. But "How you feel" questions are less threatening to your teen and help spark communication.

- ◉ **Active listening.** Try restating what your child just told you, without interjecting advice or passing judgment. (For more details on this communication model, see "Key 6.") Compare Conversation 1 to Conversation 2. Notice that the second choice is more positive and can open the door to communication.

Son: I hate my English composition class, and I don't see the point in taking it. It's not like I'm gonna be a writer someday.

Conversation 1

Dad: I don't want to hear another complaint out of you— English is a requirement. Now go to your room and do your homework.

Son: This is so lame. I can't wait till I'm on my own and don't have to put up with stupid rules.

Conversation 2

Dad: I hear you—writing can be hard. But, you know, I've noticed that your grades have improved this year. Is there any way I can help?

Son: I have to write a two-page theme paper tonight. Got any suggestions for a topic?

Key 4: Control Your Anger

Many parents fail to acknowledge the extent of their anger. What's more, the parents expect their teenager to exhibit a maturity level that he or she has not yet attained.

A father may harshly command his teen, "You will not speak to me that way. That is disrespectful, and I won't put up with it." The teen walks away and the father has "won" the argument. Yet the father has exhibited the very behavior that he does not allow his teen to show. Slowly, the parent and teen relationship deteriorates.

Listening is the only constructive way to process anger. As you become a better listener, your teen will begin to feel understood. He or she may not agree with you but will respect you because you have treated him or her as a person. Your teen will be more inclined to follow your leadership.

Rather than denying anger, a parent should try to deal with anger more constructively. How? In his book *Surviving Adolescence,* here's what Larry E. Dumont, M.D., suggests:

Back off. When you feel yourself getting angry, stop. Don't try to talk out your anger with your child. Instead, wait until you've calmed down and then begin the discussion.

Think. Why are you angry with your teenager? Is it something he or she did, or are you really mad at yourself for something you failed to do?

Understand your emotions. Anger is often the result of several powerful, emotional responses: fear that your teen may get hurt, disappointment that he or she is not successful, frustration over your teen's and your inability to make a quick change, and embarrassment over failing as a parent. These emotions, while understandable, often prevent parents from finding constructive solutions.[4]

Key 5: Be Flexible

It's easy to approach your teens with tunnel vision. You know what you want and that's all you see. Unfortunately, tunnel vision will make you completely unaware of the needs of your teen. And that's how many family arguments get started—with people screaming demands at each other, blind to the needs of the others involved.

Here's the pattern. Let's say your son wants to go to the basketball game. So he approaches you.

Son: Mom, can I have the car tonight to go to the basketball game?

You: No, I need the car to go to the church board meeting tonight.

Son: You have meetings at the church nearly every other night of the week. Why can't I have the car just once?

You: Because it's my car!

An argument could be avoided. But when you have tunnel vision and can't see the other person's needs, you don't see alternatives that both parties would accept. If you don't listen, you only focus on the building emotion. *I don't need this,* you tell yourself. *My son is being disrespectful and this will stop right now.* But before you know it, the two of you are screaming at the tops of your lungs.

So what could you do? Now's the time to put your communications skills to work and find something mutually agreeable. Maybe you could suggest your teen drop you off at church, then arrange for someone else to bring you back. Or, if the meeting lasts long enough, your teen may be able to pick you up himself—even if that means that he has to leave the game a little early to get you. Or, as mortifying as it may sound to your young person, you could arrange to do just the opposite, dropping him or her off at the game.

In order for families to stay close and enjoy a fairly consistent level of harmony and unity, parents must be flexible. In his book *Growing Wise in Family Life,* Chuck Swindoll advises parents of teenagers:

> When it comes to raising teenagers, *rigidity is lethal.* Parents who refuse to flex, who insist on everything remaining exactly as it was in earlier years can expect their kids to rebel. But parents who are secure and mature enough to give ground, provide space, allow room, listen more than lecture, release tight control, maintain a calm and affirming attitude and good sense of humor can look forward to some of the most invigorating and adventuresome years in all of life.[5]

Key 6: Make "Shared Meaning" Your Goal

Here's the scene: It's Tuesday night and your daughter and you are in a heated discussion about why you won't let her attend a party on Friday night. Suddenly, she pops off with a stinging remark—"You *never* care about what I want, you're just out to drive me crazy all the time!"—followed by a long list of gripes . . . like the time when she was 12 months old and *you* took away her favorite squeaky toy, then made her eat strained asparagus.

At this point, the two of you are steamed—and nothing is getting resolved.

If you're tired of pointless arguments with your teenager that never seem to accomplish anything—except maybe your blood pressure rising and him or her being grounded—try a communication style called shared meaning. Here's how it works:

◉ Your daughter was bugged that you wouldn't let her go to a party with her friends on Friday night, so she stormed up to her bedroom and slammed shut the door. You want to diffuse the situation, so you approach her and say, "Could we please talk about this. I'd like you to hear my side."

◉ Once she agrees to hear you out, you explain your point of view (which you've thought through ahead of time) without being interrupted. "Look, I know attending this birthday party is important to you, but I don't know this girl or her parents . . . and I don't like the idea of you staying out past midnight at a stranger's house. If you can give me some more information—such as what's going to happen at this party and who is going to be there—maybe we can work something out. Understand?"

◉ Next, your daughter repeats her interpretation of what she just heard you say. "You just don't like these people because they don't attend our church and they live in a poor neighborhood."

◉ You then clarify or confirm what she said, ensuring that she has accurately understood your thoughts and feelings. "No, that isn't what I said, now is it? I told you I need more information about this girl, her parents, and exactly what's going to happen at this party. If you share more information, maybe we can work something out."

◉ The process continues with your teen sharing her point of view. You listen and then repeat what she said.

The goal of shared meaning is to be heard *accurately*. And once you've had a chance to state your case and listen to your teen's perspective, the foundation is set for communication—and for a fair solution to what's bugging you.

Communication tip: Make eye contact with your teen when you talk with him or her. True, this can be hard, especially when you're upset. But looking away or ignoring your teen when he or she is trying to talk to you is perceived as disinterest.

Also, follow this checklist:

- Think before you speak.
- Listen without interrupting.
- Avoid a judgmental tone of voice.
- Speak calmly without raising your voice.
- Talk to your teen in a way you want him or her to talk with you.

With determination and practice, your communication skills will improve. Remember, good communication keeps doors open, but bad communication may cause you to get doors slammed in your face.

Tune In

Get your teen to open up by . . .

- analyzing the character qualities every parent should possess.
- exploring ways you can meet these needs.

Let's begin with an experiment. In the space below, jot down the most damaging and negative aspect of your life, the last thing you'd ever tell anybody, and the last thing you'd ever want anyone to find out about you.

Read the paragraph below *before* you begin to write.

OK . . . I'll shoot straight with you. I really don't expect you to write damaging information about yourself in the box above. But do jot down a description of the kind of person with whom you would share the worst possible thing about yourself. Don't give the name of a person, make a list of the qualities this person must possess.

Here's what I wrote: Confidentiality, loving spirit, godly, kind, nonjudgmental, compassionate, accepting, patient, understanding, willing to listen, and above all . . . trustworthy.

I believe these are the most important character qualities of a parent. You probably included other great qualities that I left off this list. If you want your teen to open up to you, and, especially, to come to you for help, you need to (1) be the kind of person your teen is willing to go to, and (2) put yourself in your teen's shoes.

Suppose your young person has some deep, dark, horrible secret eating away at him or her and just can't live with it any longer. Your son or daughter needs help to resolve the issue and knows he or she needs to share every slimy detail with you.

Question: Will your child come to you with this problem or will he or she be too afraid of being judged or disappointing you? If your teen would be afraid, what can you begin doing to become the type of person your child would confide in? What specific skills from this chapter can you begin using to communicate with your teenager?

Tune In Challenge

1. In the space provided, write . . .
Your strengths as a parent:

What you want to improve:

2. Read Phil. 2:1-11. How can imitating Christ's example of humility open doors to better communication with your teen?

3. Pray daily for your relationship with your teen. You probably already pray for your teen on a daily basis. But do you ever pray about your relationship? Ask Jesus to help you break down communication barriers, build bridges of understanding, and help you develop the character qualities your teen needs in a parent.

Invade Your Teens' World
(Without Invading Their Space)

"I'm sick of being a wimpy Christian," 15-year-old Jason confessed to his buddies in his discipleship group. "I act one way at church and around you guys, then another way with my friends at school. It's like . . . I don't even know who I am at times."

Jason's comments had struck a nerve with the four other boys lounging on my living room floor. Chris and Andy, both 16, nodded their heads in agreement, and 14-year-old Brian—who was busy all evening stuffing his face with chips—perked up too.

"I know God doesn't like it when I act this way," Jason continued. "And I know I need to give up a few bad friendships so I can grow stronger as a Christian. But it's really hard."

Suddenly, a serious expression washed across Brian's face. "I'm with you, Jason," he said. "I've been a wimp with my faith. I've got some stuff to change in my life too."

Just as I was about to jump in with a few words of encouragement, Chad—one of the older guys in the group—spoke up. "You're on the right track," the 17-year-old said. "Lose those friendships that are pulling you down. That's what I had to do.

"I used to care more about popularity than my faith," Chad continued. "Then one day I realized it's stupid to follow the crowd at school. I'm a Christian. I'm different . . . and that's OK."

I sat back and watched with amazement. *These guys are*

spurring each other to a deeper walk with Christ, I thought. *My boys are growing up!*

Every Tuesday night I disciple five teen guys from my church's youth group. We call ourselves the Breakaway Boyz. It had taken three years for my discipleship group to reach a deep level of unity, openness, and trust . . . three years of Bible studies, praying together, and crying with each other (not to mention all the pizza pig-outs, video marathons, and squirt-gun wars we'd shared).

My goal as a discipler is to help each teen . . .

◎ give up his own will for God's will.

◎ live daily a life of spiritual sacrifice for Christ's glory.

◎ strive to consistently obey our Lord.

Our goal as parents should be the same. Let's look at how we can accomplish this.

Love + Relationship + Time = Parenting a Teen

A few months back I received a letter from a young man named Eric. He wrote, "Problems with drugs, alcohol, and premarital sex happen among teens—even among Christian youth—when they aren't happy with themselves. They're desperately searching for self-worth. All along, the answer is right in front of them: Jesus."

Eric is absolutely right. Young people are hungry for something to commit their lives to. They yearn for parents and youth workers who will help them find purpose in life. You have the answer.

But affecting the life of a modern teen doesn't mean you have to suddenly become superhuman or a rock star or even a pyrotechnics expert. (Merely entertaining teens is out of the question.) Instead, just step into their world and show you care.

That's what Jesus did, and He was the ultimate discipler. Those who followed Christ ended up being served by Him. (Imagine that—the Creator serving His creation!) His disciples also got a big dose of encouragement, mixed with some well-deserved correction from time to time. Jesus stretched His disciples as they struggled to receive the truth and to obey God's will.

Want to have a greater impact on your teen? Follow Christ's example.

How to Reach Out

To make your children happy, you do not have to spend extravagantly or give them the biggest and the best. In fact, the simpler, the better. Listen to what 13-year-old Brady says on this topic: "I know my mom loves me because of the countless little things she does for me. She sews buttons on my shirt when they fall off and she helps me with my homework every night. All these things spell *love.*"

Fifteen-year-old Michelle appreciates the material things she gets from her parents, but she prefers their attention. "My parents have given me everything I have," she said "In my mind, that's love. They have given me not only the essentials but far more than I need. But the thing that means most is the time they spend with me."

Teens need affection from their parents. They need positive affirmation, emotional support, nurture and, most of all, they need their parents' time.

Time and Importance

We spend time in the areas of life that are most important to us. That's a significant concept, and our teens have picked up on it. They might as well have put it in a formula like this:

Time Spent + Interest + Commitment = Love

Face it, your kids see where you spend your time. If you don't spend time with them, they quickly get the message: they're not important. When 17-year-old Mandy was asked, "How do you know your parents love you?" she responded, "Because they're always there for me. I can talk to them about anything. I know they'll take the time to listen and to help me solve a problem—instead of shoving me aside."

Quality and Quantity

The statement "quality time is much better than quantity time" is wrong. Your child, like your spouse, needs a lot of your time. When you short-change your teen, you short-change yourself.

For example, consider your favorite meal. If you were limited to a tiny nibble of your favorite food, without quantity, would its quality still please you? I doubt it. You wouldn't agree that quality food is better than quantity food—especially if you were starving! To some degree, the fast-food mentality represents what some American teens get from their parents.

Popular author and youth speaker Bill Sanders explains: "Sometimes Mom or Dad wants the same quality, but quicker service, faster times together—'I'll take the hamburger now, instead of in ten minutes. Even though it won't be fresh off the grill, that's OK, because I have an important appointment a few minutes from now.' Fast-food parenting doesn't have a lot of benefits."[1]

A healthy balance of quality and quantity time is the key. This involves giving your teen your undivided attention—whether you're talking to each other, playing a game, or doing a project together. And for most of us, teens and adults alike, nothing is more important than the focused attention of those we love.

Young people know that love shown by parents says, "Your life is important, daughter [or son], and I'm going to give you my time." When you spend time with them, show them you will listen and talk and work things out together.

Sixteen-year-old Jonathan was asked, "On a zero to ten scale, how much do your parents love you?" Without batting an eye he answered, "Ten." When I asked why he felt so strongly, he said, "Well, for one thing, they tell me. But most important of all, they show me every day!

"Even though my dad's military career keeps him pretty busy—he's in charge of 200 people and often gets called away in the middle of the night—he makes family time a priority. When he's home, it's like my mom and sister and I have his full attention. As a family, we always do stuff together. And both my mom and dad really seem interested in what's going on in my life."

What Jonathan said next really caught my attention: "I'd say the most important message teens need to hear from parents is, 'I love you.' And the most important action they need to see is a mom and a dad getting into their lives and spending time with them."

Here are some suggestions to help you balance your time properly, express your love, and invade their world (without invading their space):

Share some "crazy" times. Don't let your teen take a back-seat in your busy schedule. Clear your calendar on weekends and have some fun. A simple change of pace is a great stress-reliever, and memories you make will last a lifetime.

Not sure what to do? The possibilities are endless: have dinner in a fancy restaurant, attend a hockey game, try go-carting, go to a spa. One mom made reservations at a hotel for herself and her 15-year-old daughter, then spent all day shopping and half the night watching movies, eating junk food, and talking.

Take an interest in your teen's world. Think about your teenage years. What was important to you? The things that meant a lot to you—getting a good grade on your math test, finding a group of friends, making the team—are similar to the things that are important to your teen right now.

Invite them into *your* world. The teens I work with love to hear about my job and the pressures I face as an adult. They also enjoy looking at—or rather *laughing* at—my old yearbooks.

Letting them into my world often sparks some pretty good discussion starters about generational differences and the kinds of problems I dealt with as a teen. In turn, the teens open up about what's bugging them.

Affirm them daily. Teens need to regularly hear words of encouragement from their parents. Fourteen-year-old Melissa, who recently broke her arm, received some much-needed affirmation at just the right time, "I know that my parents love me because while I was having such a hard time keeping up with my schoolwork, they encouraged me. They never forced me to do homework when I wasn't feeling well but told me that I could do it later. They said how proud they were that I was trying so hard."

Consider this: When teens have the courage to share something intimate, what are they looking for initially? Acceptance and affirmation. If you confess to God, what do you get? Acceptance and affirmation.

> For we do not have a high priest who is unable to sympathize with our weaknesses, but we have one who has been tempted in every way, just as we are—yet was without sin. Let us then approach the throne of grace with confidence, so that we may receive mercy and find grace to help us in our time of need *(Heb. 4:15-16).*

Do you want your teen to confide in you? Imitate how Christ treats us during confessional moments.

Build up his or her faith daily. "The paint is still wet, and you're still under construction. But take a good, hard look in the mirror. God's creating a masterpiece in you!"

I try to instill that important bit of encouragement in the teens I work with—especially when they blow it in their walk with Christ. Though most teens know God always forgives, their hearts don't grasp how much God is on their team.

God isn't shaking His finger at us when we blow it. Instead, He picks us up, dusts us off, encourages us to keep trying, and points us onward and upward. That's how grace works for the believer—it motivates us to keep moving. We grind to a halt when we don't understand His grace.

Hug them often. How long has it been since you've wrapped your arms around your teenager and held him or her—just because? We should abundantly give hugs, kisses, and tender touches. Yet too many parents pull back when their kids enter adolescence. True, you need to be more sensitive about the times when you give hugs—showing affection to your teen at the mall, for example, is probably off-limits—but make sure you give a daily dose of physical touch.

Be vulnerable. Don't be afraid to admit your weaknesses. It's OK to admit your actions don't always match your convictions. Too often, we think that by saying the words, "I blew it," we're somehow weaker. Actually, just the opposite is true. A teenager admires someone who has the courage to admit his or her mistakes.

Pray daily for your kids. When a situation seems hopeless with your teen, when you feel as if you're at your wit's end, remind yourself of a few facts:

- ☉ **Prayer is powerful.** It's intimate communication with our eternal God. Imagine that! The Creator of the universe welcomes us into His presence. And He is concerned about every detail of our lives—especially the pressures of parenting a teenager.

- ☉ **Prayer is a gift from the Lord and the work of the Holy Spirit.** It's the key to being empowered and is the cornerstone of a healthy, dynamic Christian home.

- ☉ **Prayer is the single most effective tool to reach**

youth. After all, God is the One who changes lives. His love for your child is far beyond your comprehension. Release your teen to our Heavenly Father in prayer, and trust that He will lead your young person through the topsy-turvy teen years.

LESSON FROM THE TRENCHES

How You Can Be a Role Model

by Cheryl Sloan Wray[2]

Sandy looked at her 15-year-old daughter, Morgan, with frustration. Sandy knew the look on Morgan's face—something was bothering her. Sandy assumed it concerned a report Morgan had due for science class. "Not that I would know about that," Sandy muttered.

She tried to find out more. "Is anything wrong, honey?" she asked.

"Not really," Morgan answered. "It's nothing important."

"Let me know if I can help."

"Sure, Mom," Morgan tried to smile. "But I think I'll call Jake. He might be able to help me."

Sandy winced at the words. She was thrilled that Morgan could go to Jake, their church's youth group leader, but wished he wasn't always her daughter's problem solver.

Why can't I be my daughter's friend and role model? she asked herself.

🌀 ﾚ ﾟ ℘

As the parent of a teen, you've probably wondered the same thing. Why won't your young person ask you for advice? Why doesn't he or she seem to value your opinion or place trust in what you say?

You seem to be a role model for your coworkers, your unchurched friends, even some of the other children and teenagers you know. Why can't you experience this with your own child?

There's a comforting answer: You can be your teen's role model. It just takes a little understanding and some hard work.

What Is a Role Model?

When we say someone serves as a role model, we mean the individual is someone others admire or try to emulate. For teenagers this often means the person is someone they want to be like—whether it's because of the person's lifestyle, athletic prowess, or the attitudes the person shows.

Some of those role models are celebrities out of your teen's reach (athletes and movie stars), while others are in his or her own circle of influence (youth ministers, teachers, and other parents). What do those people have that make them attractive to your teen?

What Teens Crave

Why do teens look up to the other adults in their lives? What about a person makes him or her a role model to your teen?

Whether or not we like it, parents are sometimes considered the enemy. Teenagers see their moms and dads as judgmental and unconcerned about their lives. Two qualities, therefore, are very important in being a role model.

1. A role model is understanding, not condescending. When 13-year-old Jenny seemed especially upset about a boy not liking her at school, her father said, "That's nothing to worry about. You're too young to even think about boys." When the dad spoke those words, he was telling Jenny that her concerns were not important. Yet it was very serious in her 13-year-old world.

Role models try to connect with a teen in order to understand what he or she is going through. They do so without belittling the teen's problems or downplaying the teen's triumphs.

2. A role model is a friend, but also a leader. We often think that to be a role model to our teenager we must know the name of every new movie or be able to use teenage slang. That's not necessarily true.

While most role models understand the teen's life and act friendly, they also take on a leadership role with the teen. Role models provide answers or suggestions in the teen's struggles and give insights to the teen about their own experiences.

How Parents Can Be Good Role Models

You, the mother or father, can become a role model to your teenage child in many ways. Here are two keys that are the skills behind good parenting.

◉ **Be available.** Let your teenager know you are available. While your son or daughter may not beat down your door every time he or she has a question or has something wonderful to share, your teen is more likely to do so if you have left that door open.

Say something like, "I'm always here for you" or "I'd love to hear about your day." Don't apply pressure, but let your teen know you are there for him or her.

◉ **Listen to your teen.** Being available to your teenager does not mean listening with one ear and then giving a long string of advice.

Listen to your teen first, asking plenty of follow-up questions. Don't jump in with advice (even when you clearly see what should be done). Instead, proceed slowly, asking your teen what he or she thinks should be done.

◎ ⸖ ⸕ ⸙

Being a role model to your teenage son or daughter may seem to be an impossible undertaking. But realize that your young person needs someone just like you—someone who loves him or her and who can point in the right direction.

Parent and Teen Hot Spots

"Why do I get blamed for *everything!*" your daughter screams.

You cross your arms and lock eyes with her. "Watch your tone, young lady," you say sternly. "You're not *always* blamed, but you are the oldest in this family, and you know better. I want you to set a good example."

Your 13-year-old son, who had taken cover behind you earlier, secretly gets your daughter's attention, sticks out his tongue, and grins from ear to ear.

"Did you see that?" your daughter gasps. "Maggot is doing it again."

"Oh, give it a rest," you respond. "Why can't you two get along? Why do you turn our house into a battle zone?"

Your daughter gasps again. Just before slamming her bedroom door, she launches one last missile: "You and Dad let him get away with murder."

Inside her room, your teen daughter buries her face in her pillow. She's convinced that you conceived her little brother just to spy on her.

"He's like a miniature KGB agent," your daughter grumbles. "Just when I thought I could trust him, he tells Mom what I did last week—and I get grounded for the next three years. I saw that smile when he heard me get in trouble. If I could just get my hands on those lips . . ."

◎ ≶ ⚡ ⚡

Your son flops on his bed and throws a Nerf ball against his Colorado Rockies poster.

"'No-o-o-o-o,'" he mumbles in his best prison warden voice. "'You *can't* have that, you *can't* go there, you *can't* hang out with those friends!' Mom and Dad think I still wear Pampers. When will they learn I'm *not* a little kid anymore?"

During supper he barely says two sentences—one if you don't count, "Pass the potatoes—please." Later, after his homework is completed, he doesn't watch TV with the family. Instead, he shuts his bedroom door and loses himself in his CDs.

Meanwhile, you collapse in the easy chair and squeeze shut your eyes. You replay the argument in your head and wonder, *Why do we go through this every time I say the word "No." Why do I always come off as the prison warden? Why can't we have a peaceful relationship?*

◉   ≋   ⚷   ☺

These are familiar scenes between teenagers and their parents, yet I can't help but wonder. . . .

How can a houseful of people who love each other so much sometimes feel as if they can't stand each other?

How can we live under the same roof with our spouses, sons, and daughters, and know all of their strange quirks, yet sometimes feel like complete strangers?

An emotional war has erupted between many parents and teens. This is a perfectly normal phase of growing up that psychologists describe as the war of independence. With each step young people take on the path to adulthood, they become more independent of their mothers and fathers.

In the meantime, how can you survive the daily storms on your home front? And what can you do to cool down the hot spots and even improve your relationship with your teens? Here are a few ideas:

- ◉ **Understand the battle.** Teenagers are very sensitive about personal injustice, self-worth, independence, privacy, and love. And whether or not they admit it, they're actually looking for boundaries. Some of their testing behavior is a way of saying, "Do you care enough about me to keep me from doing this stupid thing? Do I have your attention? Are you concerned about who I am and what I'm doing?"

- ◉ **Allow for a cooling-off period.** Unless you detect some serious disrespect, a little bit of the cold-shoulder treatment from your teen won't hurt. True, it doesn't feel too good, but he or she needs a chance to cool off and to process the situation. For that matter, you need to cool off as well. Give your teen time to cool off, but . . .

- **Don't let your teen shut down for too long.** Too much of the cold-shoulder treatment could cause even more tension later on. After a fair amount of time has passed, try to get your teen talking about the disagreement. As you communicate and listen, you will ultimately open the doors to greater understanding.

- **Let your teen know he or she is on your most wanted list.** Say something like this: "If you feel you're on our most wanted list, you're *right!* Regardless of all the hot spots we'll experience together, we really *want* you. We really do *love* you."

In the rest of this chapter, let's focus on four basic home front hot spots: sibling rivalry, teenage friendships, media choices, and school performance. We'll examine the intricacies of each of these tension zones, as well as solutions to those tiring fights.

Remedy Sibling Storms

You know sibling rivalry is a fact of family life—a difficult fact that can intensify the moment your teen hits puberty. Yet few things can cause a parent to become a raving maniac quicker than constant bickering.

So, what's the answer? Is it possible to diffuse the constant missiles your children launch at each other? Can you actually teach your teenage son or daughter to be a peacemaker?

While you'll never eliminate sibling rivalry, you can improve your teen's attitude and save *your* sanity.

This all begins with a heart-to-heart conversation.

- **Help them avoid a "bitterness burn."** Tell them: "Bitterness hurts you far more than it hurts others. It's like a hot coal. The longer and tighter it is held, the deeper the burn. Bitterness can leave scars that even time cannot erase."

- **Encourage them to fight their own battles.** Tell them: "Don't report every little disagreement to me. Sit down

with whoever wronged you and figure out how to settle
the conflict. As you confront your brother or sister, avoid
finding out whose fault it is. Instead, find a solution to
your problem."

◉ **Teach them to forgive . . . then forgive again.** Tell
them: "Think of all the ways you feel you have been
wronged by your brother or sister, then work toward genuinely forgiving. Forgiveness is not denying that you've
been hurt or trying to understand why a person has acted
a certain way. Genuine forgiveness involves consciously
choosing to release the hurt someone has caused—and
continuing to love that person. Can you get to this point
with the family member who has wronged you?"

Nurture Their Friendships

"Give me a break!" Matt blurts. He rolls his eyes and slumps
on the couch. "I'm not a little kid anymore. I can handle myself. Besides, my new friends aren't as bad as you think."

His father takes a deep breath and looks him in the eyes.
"I'm just saying that friends can have a big influence on us.
Don't let these guys talk you into doing something you'll regret."

"Dad—the world is different now," Matt insists. "The whole
peer pressure thing is so outdated. No one pushes you into doing anything these days. If anybody suggests something you
don't want, you just say no. That's it. They leave you alone."

Matt's father raises a suspicious eyebrow as his son darts toward the door.

"I'll be home by 10. And don't worry," Matt assures him. "I'll
be fine!"

A few minutes later, Matt crawls into a car packed with other guys his age. "So—what mall are we going to?" he asks.

The driver laughs. "Mall? Yeah, right!"

The sarcasm in his voice bothers Matt—not to mention the
three unfamiliar guys crammed into the backseat staring at him.

This is the second Saturday this month that the plans have
"suddenly changed." Driving aimlessly around town, drag rac-
ing cars at every stoplight, yelling at pedestrians and hanging
out at a convenience store isn't Matt's idea of having fun. Besides, his buddy's canned lines are becoming vaguely familiar:

"If I'd known earlier that the guys had other ideas, I'd have told you. And how was I supposed to know that they were gonna pocket some stuff at the store? Listen—nobody forced you to come with us."

Matt swallows hard and shakes his head, his mind wandering back to his dad's warning. Suddenly, he decides to speak up: "You're right. I don't have to be here. So let me out at that corner—*now!*"

After a shrug and a slam of the door, the car speeds into the night.

Matt pops a couple of quarters into the pay phone and clears his throat. "Dad, about those new friends of mine. . . ."

Standing up to peers who do dumb things is one of the bravest —and toughest—steps a teenager can take. And the more your children stand up to peer pressure, the stronger they'll become. How can you prepare them for peer pressure?

- **Help them set standards and consider their actions before they get into a tight spot.** Help your teens understand it's better to stand alone, knowing they did the right thing, than to feel like "one of the crowd," realizing they broke their word to themselves and to God.

- **Steer your kids to the right pack.** Encourage them to surround themselves with friends who share their values. Show them why it's important to spend less time with guys and girls who aren't interested in pursuing a godly walk.

- **Create an environment of trust.** Let them know that, in times of trouble, you're there for them.

Unplug the Media Wars . . .

The latest Schwarzenegger-meets-Stalone, shoot-'em-up, thrill-a-minute flick is exploding on the big screen, and your daughter can't wait to gobble up the action with her friends (which means her guy friends, of course).

"All my friends are gonna see it," she says. "Can I go?"

"What's it rated?" you ask.

Suddenly, lightning flashes behind you and ominous organ music fills the room. Then silence.

Your daughter swallows hard and nervously shifts her eyes. You can practically see the wheels spinning inside her head. *So, what's her response this time? The usual?*

"Look," she says, "it has a few explosions, OK?" *Yep, it's the usual.*

"It's not PG and it's not suitable for little kids—I'll admit that," she continues. "But I'm *not* a little kid anymore. I can handle it, Mom."

You take a deep breath and fold your arms, bracing yourself for Media War No. 1,466,392. You ask yourself, *Does it always have to erupt into a fight? Isn't there a better way?*

◉   ⸙   ⚲   ☙

Popular media is one of the biggest sources of conflict between parents and teenagers. I often get letters from teens that go something like this: "I wish my parents would ease up. After all, it's just a _____." (Insert the word of your choice—*song, computer game, TV show, movie.*)

The fact is, we live in a mixed-up world of high-tech toys and low-tech values, and it's taking a toll on many families. Too many households—including Christian ones—have tuned in the voices of today's self-centered, "greed and trash" culture, and tuned out the ultimate truth—God's Holy Word.

Like most parents, you're probably weary from the constant battles, but I urge you to hold your ground. Here are some suggestions:

1. Help Your Teens Evaluate Their Media Diet

The key is to help them know *why* being picky with the press (and the movies and the music) is important, *what* to be picky about, and then *taking a stand* for what's right.

Use Phil. 4:8 as a guide to what's entering their eyes and ears: "Finally, brothers, whatever is true, whatever is noble, whatever is right, whatever is pure, whatever is lovely, whatever is admirable—if anything is excellent or praiseworthy—think about such things."

2. Encourage Them to Ask Hard Questions

◉ **Is it *true*?** Does this movie mock what God says is good?

- **Is it *noble?*** Does this book help me develop a proper mind-set?
- **Is it *right?*** Does this TV program cause me to compromise biblical truths?
- **Is it *pure?*** Does this concert offer more trash than treasure to make it worth my time and money?
- **Is it *lovely?*** Would I be embarrassed if my youth leader found out I read this magazine?
- **Is it *admirable?*** Does this song offer wisdom and/or benefit me in any way?
- **Is it *excellent?*** Is this the best possible way for me to spend my time?
- **Is it *praiseworthy?*** Am I drawn closer to God because of it?

3. Tell Them "You Are What You Eat"

Every song, book, and movie has a philosophy. Some are into hedonism ("Get high, have sex, and party hardy!"). Others preach politics ("Kill the cops and overthrow the system!"). Still others promote pessimism and despair ("Life is meaningless!"). Obviously, the argument "It's just harmless entertainment . . . it doesn't affect me," simply isn't true.

Break Bad Study Habits

Your son takes his seat in fourth-period science and then gasps. Three spine-tingling words are scribbled boldly across the chalkboard: *Exam this Friday!*

"Nooooo!" he screams. "Not another test!"

The lights darken and glowing green mists rise from the floor. His teacher—Dr. Jekyll—hunches over your boy's desk, wringing his hands. "That's right . . . a test. And it will cover the first 1,000 chapters, along with my endless lectures on the rare snails of Kilimanjaro. HA, HA, HA, HA!"

Thunder claps . . . and your son wakes up.

He bolts out of bed and throws off the covers. "Whew!" he mumbles to himself. "It was just a dream. Just a crazy nightmare of a . . ." He stops in midsentence, and his eyes grow big.

"Wait a second. I *do* have a test in fourth-period science. It's today . . . and I'm gonna (gulp) fail! Arrrgggghhhh!"

◉ ≋ ≴ ☌

As school rolls around each year, most teenagers panic.

Homework assignments stack up, and term papers are put off until the last possible second. Cram sessions for "tomorrow's big test" become normal. "Sleep?" your teen says with a nervous twitch. "I'll catch up on that at Christmas . . . or maybe spring break!"

You can help your teen correct bad study habits, steer clear of the "failure cycle," and get off on the right foot. Start with the following tips.

Tune in the teacher. If your teen is constantly thinking about grand-slam home runs, triple-decker burgers, or cheerleading practice, he or she isn't getting what the teacher is saying. Three simple steps will maximize his or her classroom time. Tell your teen this:

- ◉ Remind your brain to concentrate each time it wants to wander.
- ◉ Take notes on what the teacher says, as well as on your reading assignments. Review your notes several nights before a test.
- ◉ Ask your teacher questions about the things you don't understand.

Don't procrastinate. What a concept! Yet most members of the teenage species just don't seem to get this. Tell your son or daughter, "If your teacher assigns 15 pages of reading every night for a week, read each section each night. Don't let it amass into a festering heap, like your gym socks, until you have to read 75 pages during the weekend." Remind him or her that wise teens attack their homework daily, so it won't end up attacking them. One key to doing this is to get organized with a daily planner. Writing down all assignments—along with due dates—will help your teen stay on track.

Test insurance. Whether your son or daughter is dealing with a case of "test-taking jitters" or the fear of giving an oral report, remind your teen that God is near: "The LORD will keep you from all harm—he will watch over your life; the LORD will watch over your coming and going both now and forevermore" (Ps. 121:7-8).

How One Dad Ended His Son's Angry Outbursts[1]

His eyes were set, his chin was protruding, his arms were flailing, and his voice was 20 decibels too high. But his words hurt most.

"You don't understand. You don't *ever* understand. You don't even *try* to understand."

With that final angry outburst, 15-year-old Derek stormed out the front door, leaving his frustrated dad, Gary, standing in the living room, feeling foolish. Derek would be back, and there would be another "conversation" . . . and yet another explosion. At least that had been the pattern for several months.

Is this teenage anger normal? Should teens be allowed to scream at their parents? Most important, how do you stop it?

"I always screamed back during our arguments," Gary says. "I didn't know what else to do. I tried other acts of discipline, like taking away privileges, but the anger seemed to mount. Every explosion seemed hotter than the one before."

But on this particular day, Gary couldn't shake off his son's remarks. "You don't understand. You don't ever understand." He knew the first two statements were true. He certainly did not understand what was going on inside his teenage son. But he thought he was trying to bridge the gaps.

"I tried to be a responsible parent," Gary says. "I didn't want to raise a son who screamed at people when he didn't get his way. I could not accept his angry outbursts. But I didn't know how to stop them."

Gary did know one thing: Arguing with his son was not helping the situation. Something needed to be done—immediately!

As this Oklahoma dad began to analyze his own behavior, he made a connection. "I discovered that when I feel angry, it's almost always because I believe someone has treated me unfairly," Gary says. "In fact, my own anger toward my son was based on *his* behavior, which I viewed to be inappropriate. *He should not be screaming at me,* I reasoned. *That is wrong.* Thus, I felt angry."

Gary soon concluded that his son's anger was from the same source. Derek became angry because he felt Gary did not treat him fairly. Legitimate or "perceived," Gary's wrong was real in

Derek's mind, and his anger was a normal response. Because we are made in God's image, we all have a concern for fairness. Our anger is stirred when we think someone is not treating us fairly.

Now that Gary better understood his anger, he still faced the immense task of dealing with his son's outbursts. The weary dad picked up some books on the topic and learned that if teen anger is not heard by the parent, the anger will go underground and will express itself somewhere else—such as poor grades, shoplifting, drugs, sex. It is a subconscious attempt to get back at the parents, called passive-aggressive behavior. The teen becomes passive to the parent in ways such as being compliant after a big argument, but the anger appears in aggressive behavior in another area of life.

Gary thought, *Fortunately, my son's anger has not yet gone underground. He is still screaming at me! Maybe I can learn to listen and help him process the anger.* Here is what Gary learned.

Step 1: Listen. Calmly ask questions and let your teen express the anger. The more questions a parent asks and the more intently he or she listens, the more likely the angry teen's volume will decrease.

Step 2: Get to the source. Don't just focus on the *way* your teens express anger. Seek to understand what they think is unfair or wrong. You may not agree with their perceptions, but hear them out. If they think they were wronged, the anger will not go away until they feel you have heard and understood their complaint. You are still the parent and you have the final word, but your teens need to feel you think their ideas are important.

Step 3: Promote mutual understanding. After you've had a "listening session" with an angry teen, say something like this: "I really appreciate you telling me your anger about that situation. We may not always agree, but I want you to know I always want to understand how you feel. I'm not a perfect parent and sometimes I don't make the best decisions, but I really want to do what is best for you. I hope we can both learn to express our feelings more calmly. Regardless of the way you express your feelings, I always want to hear them and what you think.'"

Gary says if you're used to arguing with your teen, perhaps you can break the pattern by saying, "I've thought about our relationship and I realize sometimes I'm not a very good listener. Often when you feel strongly about something, I also end up getting angry. I want to be a better listener. In the future, I'll try to ask more questions and really seek to understand, because I do value your ideas and feelings."

Gary is convinced a teen's anger—as well as an adult's—can be processed in genuine conversation, not in shouting matches. "It's working for me," Gary says. "I'm finally getting through to my teen."

Send Your Teens on the *Right* Course

When it came to passing down Christian values to their three daughters, Floyd and Bonnie Cox did this the right way. I know, because I married their youngest daughter, Tiffany.

My wife is now in her 30s, yet the lessons she learned as a teenager have molded her faith—and those will be passed down to our children.

Floyd and Bonnie set their children on the right path with three priorities: (1) *Church was a family priority.* They involved their kids in ministry activities from the toddler through teen years. (2) *Building confident children was a priority.* They helped their daughters comprehend their value in Christ. (3) *Setting goals for the future was a priority.* They encouraged their kids to dream big and to concentrate on their goals.

Let's focus our attention on these three ways you can send your teens on the right course in life—by nurturing a healthy self-image, motivating them to strive for excellence, and teaching them to set goals.

Nurture a Healthy Self-Image

I met Daniel at a youth event in Tampa, Florida, where I was a speaker. The 16-year-old was polite, well-spoken, and handsome. He reached out and shook my hand, then paused, trying to collect his thoughts. Something obviously bothered him.

"I'm sort of embarrassed, but I need some advice," he said, looking at the floor.

"Go ahead, Daniel," I responded. "Tell me what's on your mind."

"Well, I was wondering how I should talk to girls—considering the way I look."

I was confused. "I'm not following you, Daniel. What's wrong with the way you look?"

He glanced up, equally confused. "My face," he said. "It's all covered with zits. What girl would be interested in me? Besides, I'm not very athletic, and I'm not part of the popular crowd."

I squinted. "Oh, I see. You do have some acne. But know what, Dan? I didn't notice it. The first thing I noticed about you was your smile. Then I was impressed with your courage. It takes guts to open up to a stranger."

Daniel smiled again, and we had a heart-to-heart talk. I wanted to help him connect with reality: Despite what he's been taught, his life counts—zits and all!

The pressure Madison Avenue and Hollywood places on our society to look perfect beats up the self-esteem of our teenaged daughters. However, teen girls aren't the only ones who often feel down about themselves. Like Daniel, many boys are trapped in a lie . . .

◉ the lie that they're worthless unless they possess a bank vault bursting with bucks, have the IQ of Einstein, and are blessed with a perfect body

◉ the lie that they'll never measure up among their peers

It's time Christian young people unplug from worldly philosophies and tune into the truth of Jesus Christ.

Here are some ways you can help your teens.

Teach them their value. Start with a pep talk. Communicate this message to your teen: "God made you, and He doesn't make junk. You are a unique person with lots of ability. You are loved by your Creator. In fact, you are the Lord's work of art— physically, mentally, and spiritually."

Teach them to focus on the *right* image—Christ's. Ask your young people to think of all the time they have spent in front of a mirror combing their hair, checking out those new clothes . . . expending so much effort to find acceptance.

Then point out that Christ "had no beauty or majesty to attract us to him, nothing in his appearance that we should desire him" (Isa. 53:2). Tell them people were attracted to Jesus because His beauty was internal. His heart emanated unlimited love. The peace in His eyes drew crowds. The joy of His smile was contagious.

Teach them to talk positively about themselves. Prov. 15:4 says, "The tongue that brings healing is a tree of life, but a deceitful tongue crushes the spirit." Tell your teen to replace "I don't know how" with "It's time for me to learn." Encourage them to replace "I can't" with "I will."

Build Confident Kids

The cartoon character Bart Simpson is the ultimate underachiever. He's content with average performance, his mind focuses on instant gratification, he doesn't count the cost of his actions, and he wastes energy concocting elaborate schemes to dodge responsibilities (such as the term paper due last semester).

When it comes to goals, his head is definitely in the ozone: "I'd like to be the first human to ever skateboard on Mars. Cowabunga, Dude!"

Unmotivated. Unfocused. Unrealistic. Sound familiar? Unfortunately, Bart's world describes the world too many teenagers occupy.

Take Jason, for example, a 17-year-old I mentor. Jason has flunked out of school more than once and even got into some trouble with the law.

During a camping trip, I asked Jason, "What do you hope to accomplish during your lifetime?"

"I want to be a marine biologist," he responded, "or maybe a photographer."

"Great!" I said. "Now how can you achieve these goals?"

"Humph!" Jason grunted as he shrugged his shoulders and poked a stick in the campfire. "I don't do too well at school . . . and I don't own a camera. I dunno. But each summer my mom takes me to Florida. I think snapping pictures or working with sea animals would be cool."

I'm convinced that locked inside this boy is a future Jacques Cousteau. Jason really is bursting with potential. But he lacks direction. Without the proper spark from his parents, he could end up floundering in mediocrity—always dreaming but never doing.

I'm also convinced that the keys to motivating Jason (or even Bart) center on three crucial steps:

Fuel their imagination. Get them excited about the future and the possibilities ahead of them: the things they can experience, the places they can go, the awesome adults they can become. Encourage them to dream big and to explore a few possibilities now. (This could mean taking photography lessons, volunteering at the local zoo, joining the band, or going out for a sport.)

Help them live beyond the moment. Jason is likely to squander the present watching Nick at Nite's Godzilla Marathon at the expense of tomorrow's big exam. Help your teen realize irresponsible choices won't just result in bad grades but can also set in motion bad habits—behaviors that can end up stealing their dreams. Show them how today's choices can impact tomorrow's opportunities. Encourage them to begin setting realistic goals.

Strengthen their self-esteem. I've met gang members in Chicago who would kill (or be killed) over a street basketball game. Why? They've anchored their lives to a game and have completely disconnected themselves from reality. To these boys, winning on the court equals self-worth. Your son or daughter may not be willing to die over a basketball game. But perhaps he or she has been emotionally slammed on the court or in the classroom a few times. Perhaps your teen feels trapped in the lie that he or she will never amount to much. Help your kids see that their life is like a work of art that's still in process. Tell them God would never say, "This is who you are—and who you'll always be." Instead, Jesus says, "Just imagine what you can become."

Help Them Set Goals

Ron was a 17-year-old sports nut who'd rather play baseball than do anything else. The problem was, athletics didn't come easy for him.

It wasn't because he lacked discipline or desire. Instead, Ron struggled with cerebral palsy, a disability that often made walking a chore.

Yet the teen was determined to never let a handicap spoil his game. What's more, his dad was at his side, coaching him.

Whenever Ron would start to say, "I can't do it," his dad would build him up with a big dose of encouragement: "Never say 'I can't.' Always say 'I can,' then find another way to accomplish the task."

Ron's dad even bought the boy a left-handed glove because Ron couldn't catch with his right hand . . . and it worked. "For the first time in my life, I caught a ball," Ron explains. "Today, I'm still catching baseballs."

Ron may not play in the major leagues, but at least he's in the game. He doesn't let fear—or a physical challenge—hold him back.

His dad taught him early in life that success would come from courage, diligent effort, gallons of sweat and continual godly goal setting.

Ron learned to look for alternative ways to tackle problems and to never let a challenge get the best of him. Above all, he discovered God had given him the strength to accept life's challenges. "[God] gives me the confidence to say, 'Yes, I can,'" Ron says. "I really can accomplish any goal I set my mind on."

◎ ꙮ ꙮ ꙮ

So, what's holding your teen back from reaching his or her goals? Fear? Procrastination? A shortage of motivation? Remind him or her of Ron's words: "I can."

Also, try a goal-setting activity together. Divide a sheet of paper into two columns. On the left side, write My Goals. On the right side, write How I Will Accomplish Them. Tell your teen to dream *big* and to jot down everything he or she wants to do or learn or achieve. The sky's the limit when it comes to goals!

When the list is complete, encourage your young person to pray over it. Say something to your teen like this: "Ask God to show you which goals are part of His plan—which ones you should pursue. Then ask Him to show you how to achieve them. Over the next few weeks (or months), scratch off the goals you think aren't part of God's will for your life. Write ideas on how you think God wants you to accomplish your goals on the right side of the paper."

Tell your teen to keep this sheet of paper nearby, like above his or her desk or in a prayer journal. Ask for updates on how God is directing him or her—especially ask about how the list changes over time.

When your young person feels like giving up on a dream, remind him or her of a few awesome truths:

"You can *because God broke the chains and set you free to live in wholeness, in fullness—because you've been given fullness in Christ."*

"You can *because God gives you the confidence to take risks, to fail, and to succeed."*

"You can *because God wired you to win."*

☿ TEEN INSIGHT ☿

Striving for Excellence

Lately, I've heard the same questions from teenagers all around the country:

"I have some big dreams. How can I achieve them?"

"What does it take to stand out from the crowd and really impact this world for God?"

"I want to be all the Lord calls me to be. Where do I begin?"

Hearing these questions excites me! After all, these are important questions.

My answer usually comes in the form of a story about a young man with an Olympic dream:

Faster. The coach's words screamed through Jeremy White's head. Faster on each turn. Seventy laps. No rest.

He and the five other speed skaters looked like a long train as they raced around the 400-meter ice rink. Jeremy was tailing the lead skater, but on the next turn, the current lead skater pulled off and dropped to the rear of the pack. Then it was Jeremy's turn to pace as hard as he could with the other guys following him.

Every muscle surged with pain, and his heart pounded so hard, it hurt to breathe. *How'd I ever get nicknames like Colorado Flash or Jean-Claude Van Jeremy?*

"GO! GO! GO!" barked the coach, as Jeremy took the lead.

Jeremy shrugged off the stinging razors tearing through his quadriceps and focused on his goal: competing in the Winter Olympic Games.

Building endurance and pushing his 22-year-old body to its limit six to eight hours a day, six days a week, was the only way to get there. "But if I didn't believe it was God's will for my life," he tells other racers, "I wouldn't spend another second on the ice."

The Right Anchor

To this day, Jeremy still hasn't achieved Olympic status. But he hasn't put away his skates. "Speed skating in the Olympics is my dream," he says, "yet if I don't make it, I'll put it in the past and look forward to whatever else God has planned for me. I know everything that happens to me is for a purpose—God's purpose. And His purpose is always best."

Jeremy has anchored his life to the right goal: striving for God's best. And the discipline and commitment is paying off. Each day, his body grows stronger, his skills sharpen, and he's one step closer to fulfilling his dreams. His faith in God is deepening too. The more time this athlete spends training his spiritual life—reading the Bible, praying, and seeking God's guidance—the more God reveals himself to Jeremy.

I use Jeremy's example to communicate an important truth to teenagers: We discover God's best for our lives when we make Him the No. 1 priority of our lives.

The Right Track

◉ **Help your teen to steer clear of distractions.** Especially help them avoid the ones that will take them down a nowhere track. You know—a lust for money (instead of God's riches), an appetite for immoral sex (instead of the genuine love Christ offers), a thirst for alcohol and drugs (instead of the joy of pleasing our Creator).

◉ **Get them on an eternal track.** Just as an athlete gives his or her all to a sport, encourage your teen to give the same commitment to God.

◉ **Teach them to stay balanced.** Satan knows exactly what buttons to push! He sees your teen's weak points and goes after them. But Satan can't destroy your teen if your teen doesn't let him. Tell your child: "Christ wept for your sin, and He yearns for you to come back to Him. When you blow it, confess your sins to God and ask Him to help you get your life on the right track again."

Is Dad Missing in Action?

David sat across the table from me, his face strained with sadness. The 18-year-old had been accepted by a prestigious art college—his boyhood dream. So why the unhappiness?

David didn't sense the acceptance he cherished most: approval from his father.

"He'd accept me if I were a jock like my brother," David explained as he slumped in his seat. "I guess I don't measure up in his eyes. I can't throw a football, so Dad isn't proud of me."

Sixteen-year-old Iris hadn't seen her father in years. Since her parents' separation, her dad had drifted out of her life.

"He's never been much of a family man," Iris told me as she cradled her newborn in her arms. The unwed mother kissed her child, and then looked up at me. "I'd hoped my child would have a better life. I'd hoped he'd know his father. But it won't be that way. Just like my dad, his father drinks a lot and constantly gets into trouble."

The embarrassed teen shook her head. "It's crazy," she said. "I'd give anything for a normal life—and a normal family."

Father Hunger

David and Iris are real teens. Both have so much potential. Both are attractive, healthy, and intelligent—yet terribly broken.

These teens hunger for their fathers. And like other young

people whose dads are missing in action physically or emotionally, David and Iris ache with wounds of inferiority; wounds that may take a lifetime to heal.

"Father hunger" is one factor behind the 1999 drug epidemic in Plano, Texas, says one law enforcement officer who is trying to combat the scourge. Many of Plano's youth are getting hooked on heroin—and are dying from the drug. A policeman who patrols a local high school blames parents: "They work too hard, leave children alone too long and give them ample allowances that allow them to buy drugs. . . . They think that because their kids have beepers, they're keeping up with them."[1]

But for teenagers in other parts of the nation, Dad's absence on the home front isn't always because of work demands. It's more basic.

More than 28 percent of American children live in fatherless homes. And the number of children living apart from their dads has climbed from 5.1 million in 1960 to 16.9 million in 1996.[2]

The fallout is frightening. Take a look at these alarming statistics:

❧ The likelihood that a young male will engage in criminal activity doubles if he is raised without a father and triples if he lives in a neighborhood with a high concentration of single-parent families.[3]

❧ Children living apart from their biological fathers are up to 75 percent more likely to repeat a grade in school and 70 percent more likely to be expelled from school than children with both parents.[4]

❧ Compared to females who grow up with their fathers, females from fatherless homes are 111 percent more likely to have children as teenagers, 164 percent more likely to have a premarital birth, and 92 percent more likely to dissolve their own marriages.[5]

❧ Fatherless children are five times more likely to live in poverty than children living with both parents.[6]

And just when you thought the problem of fatherlessness couldn't get any worse, it does. This time, let's focus outside the borders of our country to the Caribbean—a region most people think of as paradise. Let's look at family life in the tiny island nation of Trinidad. (Brace yourself. It's anything but paradise!)

Shea Schwartz, a missionary to Trinidad's youth, describes

the scene: "There are five women to every man, so most men have more than one family. Boys are growing up with no direction on how to be a proper father and husband.

"Teenagers are sexually active at a very young age, and there is a serious problem with STDs. In pockets of Trinidad, a new AIDS case is diagnosed every day.

"And since 85 percent of the men age 15 to 20 have a conviction on their record, there isn't much hope for the future. Christian missionaries are working hard to give young people a new beginning through Jesus Christ, yet the workers are few and the needs are great."

Fatherhood Needs a Face

Most Americans believe they know what good fathering looks like. A TV poll conducted by ABC News in 1998 asked viewers to rank the best media fathers.[7] Americans who responded selected Bill Cosby's affable Cliff Huxtable as their ideal dad. A distant second place went to Jimmy Stewart (George Bailey in *It's a Wonderful Life*), and third place went to Hugh Beaumont (Ward Cleaver, *Leave It to Beaver*).

That same ABC News poll discovered that balancing work and family demands was a father's biggest challenge. Not surprisingly, 60 percent of those polled said spending time with their children was the best thing they could do for their children.

Bottom line: fathering involves more than just bringing a baby into the world. It involves parenting that child. Real fathers are responsible to support their children socially, financially, and emotionally.

How Boys Need Fathers

Dads, if you have a teenaged son, he is at a stage in life in which he yearns for the affirmation and companionship of an adult male mentor (preferably his father).

According to Donald M. Joy, Ph.D., professor of Human Development at Asbury Theological Seminary, at two critical periods of a boy's life when he needs a man's influence, from birth to six years old, a boy "rehearses" his masculinity from his father. Then during the teen years, a boy is released from the nest by his dad.[8] A father instinctively teaches his adolescent son how to launch confidently into manhood.

"But if a boy is abandoned by his father," Dr. Joy writes in *Becoming a Man,* "or if Dad is too busy, gone too much, is an alcoholic or is otherwise caught up in his own problems or his career, the boy can suffer seriously."[9]

Fifteen-year-old Marco is a prime example. His dad left his family when he was just five. "I can't say that I really know my father at all," Marco told me. "But I do know he has a bad reputation. People call him 'El Gato'—which means 'The Cat' because he is known for 'prowling' around with other women."

Marco paused, then added: "It's really hard growing up alone. I'd give anything for a dad who cares."

How Girls Need Fathers

Iris, the girl I wrote about earlier, is a textbook example of what can happen when a young woman is disconnected from her father. Iris yearned to rest in the safe arms of a loving dad. But what she couldn't find at home, she looked for in a relationship with a college-aged man. The result was an unplanned pregnancy—along with more pain and disappointment.

An available, loving father guides, nurtures, and strengthens the lives of teen girls in three key ways:

- ❂ *He offers a positive model of manhood.*
- ❂ *He builds his daughter's self-concept.*
- ❂ *He shapes a young lady's values.*

How would you rate your daughter's relationship with Dad? Is the young lady in your life coached by a nurturing, available father?

A Checklist for Success

Here are some ideas on how fathers can get connected with their teenagers.

Give them your full attention—on a daily basis. This means putting down the newspaper and looking them in the eye when they speak.

Spend individual time with your teen. He may treat you like an outcast and gravitate toward his friends. She may act as if she prefers her marathon phone conversation to quality time with Dad. Yet now more than ever your teen needs your guidance. Spend time alone with your son and daughter at least once a week. Shoot hoops together, take walks, grab a Coke— anything! But make sure you give your son or daughter ample opportunity to talk. And remember this: Teens want and need your attention but often just don't know how to ask for it.

Communicate the Big Four. Teens crave four important messages from their dads: "I love you," "I'm proud of you," "I trust you," "I'm here for you."

Dare to be a hero. Sure, your children look up to athletes, musicians, and movie stars, but nobody can replace their father. Get deep into their hearts. Model true godliness and servant-hood. Show your son and daughter what it means to authenti-cally follow Christ.

The Wonderful World of Mom

OK, I admit it. Wonderful doesn't exactly describe the "real world" most moms live in, right?

After all, being a mother is one of the world's most thankless jobs. Despite sacrificing your desires, not to mention quiet moments with your husband, so you can feed, clothe, nurture, and train your kids, you have to put up with bickering, grumpy moods . . . and little or no appreciation for everything you do. What's more, a mom's job description is endless: cook, cleaner, chauffeur, counselor, doctor, planner, shopper, organizer, coach, cheerleader, and candle lighter for every family member's birthday cake. (You know, the candles you remembered to light for the same loved ones who not only forgot your cake but overlooked your birthday!)

You get my point. I'm also quite sure you know another truth about motherhood: Even though you don't always receive the praise you deserve, you know the world occupied by Mom is vital to a family's health. Your influence on your children is *irreplaceable.* And like most moms, you probably wouldn't trade your job for anything. Raising confident, well-adjusted children who love God with all their hearts and who serve others is a parent's highest calling.

Yet, when it comes to raising a teenager, why do so many mothers doubt their abilities or fear they just don't measure up?

Focus on the Family president Dr. James Dobson has some thoughts on this matter. In his book *Solid Answers,* he writes: "It's a cultural phenomenon. Mothers, especially, have been blamed for everything that can conceivably go wrong with children. . . . Eighty percent of the respondents to a poll [I conduct-ed] were women, and their most frequent comment was 'I'm a failure as a mother!' What nonsense! Women have been taught to think of themselves in this way, and it is time to set the record straight."[1]

Sixteen-year-old Daniel decided to set the record straight with his mom. Oddly enough, his decision came after another Tuesday night fight.

The teen retreated to his bedroom and, as usual, slammed the door. He flopped onto his bed and buried his head into a pil-low. "I'm being smothered," he said. "She's driving me crazy with her rules. Why won't she let me grow up? Why can't I fig-ure stuff out on my own!"

Then he thought of his buddy at youth group. His friend's mom had died a few years earlier. And his friend's dad worked so hard at the office that they barely saw each other. At first Daniel thought his pal had it made—with all the freedom a guy could want. Then he thought about what his buddy said at re-treat last winter:

"Sure it's a pain when moms nag at you about stuff . . . but I'd give anything to get mine back. She always did a million lit-tle things to show how much she loved me. I really loved her too. If she were still alive, I wouldn't let a day pass without telling her that."

Suddenly, Daniel didn't feel so smothered. *OK, so I acted like a jerk. I shouldn't have yelled at Mom. I know she's looking out for me. I think she's the best mom in the world—and I gotta let her know that.*

◎ ≸ ⌀ ☖

In this chapter I want to offer some encouragement by fo-cusing on what moms do right as they launch their teenagers into adulthood and how they can begin the process of letting go of their teens.

Let's begin with a case study: the healthy relationship I have with my own mother. Let me take you back to the late '70s—my teen years—and a specific moment when I began to genuinely appreciate the "Wonderful World of Mom!"

Mom's Gift of Hope

Christmas Eve was a joyful time, a family time. So why did I feel so depressed? For one thing, Mom and I were alone.

I was 17, and my five older siblings (three brothers and two sisters) were grown up and out of the house—and unable to come home for the holidays. My father had deserted my family when I was a young boy.

Dad was an alcoholic—and Mom would never allow alcohol in our house. So about the time I was learning to ride a bike, Mom was forced to take a tough love approach: "Get help and learn to be a proper husband and a father," she had told my dad, "or follow your addiction—and lose your family. You can't have both."

My father chose his addiction. His decision broke our hearts and cracked my family's foundation. Yet in the following years, my mother was determined to mend some of the fractures and to hold our family together. I'm happy to say she succeeded. My brothers, sisters, and I share a deep bond that was nurtured by our mother.

But on this Christmas, I didn't feel very festive. I missed the chaotic Grand Central Station atmosphere that usually filled our house.

"Yep, this will be a sorry holiday," I mumbled as I slouched in a recliner and stared glumly at our Christmas tree.

Does this thing actually have branches? I wondered. Our tree was covered with so many ornaments and candy canes and popcorn strands, it was nearly impossible to see anything that was remotely sprucelike.

I squinted, noticing a brightly colored decoration I had made years earlier and a couple that my sisters had created. *Mom has saved them all,* I thought. *This tree is like a time line of our lives.*

As I followed the time line, memories flooded my mind—mostly good ones.

My eyes focused on an oddly shaped antique bulb that had been passed down from my grandmother. I thought about all the family traditions my mom had established. She was so proud of our heritage. My relatives could be traced back to England, Scotland, and Sweden.

I spotted a furry, hand-stitched reindeer my mom had made.

That triggered images of the long hours she worked cooking, cleaning, and doing everything possible to keep a roof over our heads.

Suddenly, my thoughts were interrupted by the sweet smell of chocolate, followed by Mom's warm smile.

"Let's open a gift," my mom said, handing me a cup of cocoa. "We always open one present on Christmas Eve—and this year shouldn't be any different." Before I could utter a word, she plopped a big package on my lap.

"No, Mom, let's just forget about it," I protested. "Everything's all wrong this year."

Mom lifted an eyebrow. "I'd say things are pretty right," she pointed out.

I shook my head and groaned. My mom continued talking.

"Look around you," she said. "Look at where you live, and consider the food you eat. Some people in the world don't have any of these things. And think about the people who love you—your brothers and sisters. They may not be here physically . . . but we're still a family. A strong family."

Secretly, I was tracking with everything my mom had said, but my teenage pride wouldn't let me admit it. Instead, I glanced at the package on my lap and gently began tugging at the ribbon. When the last piece of wrapping paper fell to the floor, the gift was revealed.

I looked up and gasped. "Mom, you can't afford this!"

"I'm the gift giver here . . . so I'll decide what I can and can't afford."

My mom had practically emptied her savings account on a present I had talked endlessly about for years, yet had always thought was out of reach. She had bought me a 35 mm camera, with various lenses.

"Every young journalist should learn to use a camera, right?" Mom asked.

I sat speechless, feeling as if I held more than just a camera—I held some sort of link to my future. "This is amazing!" I said as I fiddled with the gadgets.

"There's a carrying bag in the box too," Mom said. "I figure you can take this to college with you next year."

I grinned. "Mom, *you're* pretty amazing. You sacrifice so much for us. What would we do without you? Who would we be?"

Suddenly, Christmas didn't seem so empty. And from that moment, I began to see my mom differently. From that moment, my world began to make a lot more sense.

A Mother's Special Influence

That night, I unwrapped the greatest gift a teen could ever receive. Of course, I don't mean an expensive camera. I unwrapped the gift only a nurturing mother can give: hope.

Despite the hardships in our lives, my mom did everything possible to shape me into a man who could face the world with confidence. She planted seeds of faith in my life and sparked in me a vision for my future.

Let me emphasize a point I made earlier—the wonderful world occupied by Mom is vital to a family's well-being. My mom's influence on my life was *irreplaceable*—and it's the same in your home.

Here are three key ways a mother influences a teenager's life:

 Mom nurtures her kids' abilities. When I was 17, Mom bought me a camera. On other occasions, she gave me a typewriter (encouraging the writer in me) and an oil painting set (sparking the artist in me). She seemed to zero in on my talents, then looked for ways to nurture and develop them. Likewise, you share with your spouse the important role of developing your teen's abilities. You are both a *coach* and *mentor.*

A coach teaches, inspires, demands, encourages, pushes, and leads. Good coaches can create great performances in ordinary people. A mentor is a tutor and a model—a person who takes a special interest in another's life. A mentor possesses a skill to teach and a willingness to do so.

Pause for a moment and think about your son or daughter. Who is this kid? What abilities has God given him or her? Now think of ways you can nurture those talents.

Please avoid a common mistake: Keep in mind that nurturing your children's abilities doesn't mean fitting them into *your* image of who *you* think they should be. A frustrated young man once complained to me about his mother's insistence that he study accounting in college. "I don't want to be an accountant," he told me. "I want to be a musician. But she thinks I'm impractical. She thinks I'll starve if I study music. What should I do?"

My advice: "First give your desires to God. Pray about them. Next, set some goals and make a plan. Think of all the reasons why you want to study music. Then list all the things you can do with a musical career: perform in an orchestra, teach, manage a music store. If you truly possess an aptitude for music, and if you sense that your desires are consistent with God's will for your life, then it sounds as if you're on the right track. Sit down with your mom and respectfully share your thoughts and plans with her."

Bottom line—help your teen discover God's will for his or her life, and then encourage him or her to strive for excellence.

◉ **Mom is a safe harbor.** Mothers and children share a special bond—one that lasts a lifetime. Yet when the turbulent teen years hit, you can't help but feel that a mom's special connection is put on hold . . . permanently.

Hang in there. Your teens will come around. In a sense, teenagers are like boomerangs. Despite the inevitable trials you encounter almost daily, those countless moments you've invested in your kids—nurturing them, teaching them right from wrong, and preparing them for life—ultimately will pay off.

At this stage of their lives, you can find the key to your sanity in a simple message from Richard Carlson, Ph.D.: "Don't sweat the small stuff."

In his book by this title, Richard writes, "Often we allow ourselves to get all worked up about things that, upon closer examination, aren't really that big a deal. We focus on little problems and concerns and blow them way out of proportion."[2]

In other words, make peace with imperfection, pick your battles wisely, and foster an environment of peace in your household. Your teen's hairstyle or clothing choice may not appeal to you, but it probably isn't worth a World-War-III-level fight. On the other hand, stand firm when it comes to issues of morality and personal safety—and other topics that belong in the "big stuff" category.

◉ **Mom plants seeds of faith.** In 2 Tim. 1:5, Paul writes: "I have been reminded of your sincere faith, which first lived in your grandmother Lois and in your mother Eunice and, I am persuaded, now lives in you also."

Even though Timothy's mother, Eunice, was Jewish, she had married a non-Jewish man who, scholars speculate, was hostile toward the things of the Lord and didn't let him be circumcised (Acts 16:1-3). Eunice apparently shouldered the entire responsibility of raising her son in the faith; she often thanked God for the support of her mother, Lois. Right from his childhood, she made sure that she taught her son from God's Word (2 Tim. 3:15), and Timothy ended up becoming a dedicated Jewish man.

As a godly mother, you are a Eunice to your teenagers. You set the spiritual tone and provide the example and instruction your children need.

That seemingly clueless boy who leaves his dirty socks on the bathroom floor could one day change his generation for Christ because he has a God-fearing, praying mom. That moody young lady who always appears overly preoccupied with the way her jeans fit could be the next Mother Teresa (because she has a mom who focuses on the eternal). God is using you to mold your son's and daughter's character. And whether or not you realize it, they are tuned in to what you're teaching.

The Wife (and Mom) of Noble Character

Where should a mom turn to find the proper expectations for being a godly woman, a committed wife, and a good mother? To the only consistently reliable source, of course—the Holy Bible.

When I think of my mom, Prov. 31 comes to mind. This passage offers some qualities and spiritual principles that all mothers can apply. Take a look:

The Prov. 31 mother . . .

Is trustworthy (v. 10): Reliable. To be counted on. Consistent. Secure. Realistic.

Is virtuous (v. 11): Morally upright. Learns from past mistakes and keeps her principles.

Is industrious (vv. 13, 14, 28): Hardworking. Diligent. Active, busy, persistent. She hangs in there with tough tasks when her body and mind tell her to quit.

Is generous (v. 15): Unselfish. Considerate. Kindhearted. Ungrudging. Always willing to give or share.

Is wise (vv. 16, 27): Perceptive. Intuitive. Thoughtful. Shrewd. Aims for practical, God-honoring goals.

Is strong (v. 17): Stable, sure of herself. She has the ability to juggle many different tasks under pressure.

Is compassionate (v. 19): Sympathetic, responsive, and warm. Willing to offer constructive help.

Is dignified (v. 28): Stands tall with grace. Poised.

Is spiritual (v. 30): Fears God and reverences her relationship with Him above everything else.

How a Mother Gently Lets Go

If parenting a teen is all about navigating him or her from childhood to adulthood, and ultimately letting go, how can you take the trauma out of the transition and even improve your relationship with your teenager? Try loving him or her, without trying to control. Practice these keys to letting go:

❧ **Encourage independence and growth.** Praise him or her for trying new activities and taking charge of plans. Also, let your teen make small decisions. How else can he or she learn to recover from bad choices? Let your teen learn plenty from the small stuff, so he or she can avoid the cost of messing up on the big stuff.

❧ **Set an appropriate amount of rules.** If you make too many, you'll become obsessive about enforcing them. If you make too few, you'll leave too much room for your teens to fail at self-discipline.

❧ **Stay connected but don't smother.** It's up to you to know what's going on in your child's emotional, physical, social, and spiritual life. But wise moms refrain from becoming drill sergeants. In other words, they don't ask endless questions about their teen's life away from home. Why? Teens read this as a lack of trust.

It's very healthy to show an interest: "Did you have a good time at the football game?" Yet don't try to get a moment-by-moment mental replay of a teen's night out. Obviously, you can't know everything your teen does—nor should you need to.

❧ **Have a healthy perspective on life.** Understand that God is bigger than any trial that will ever come your way. While you are visionary regarding your child's needs, our Heavenly Father is the One who changes lives. Pray daily for your teen. Above all, make up your mind to trust the Lord to watch over your teen. As you stop obsessing about your role as a parent, your anxiety will probably *increase* for a time. Then it will subside.

Gradually create a plan for your life that doesn't rely on family relationships for fulfillment. As a mother, your focus has been on your family's needs. Now it's time to look in the mirror and ask a few questions: Aside from being a mom and a wife, who are you? What does God want to teach you? How else does He want to use you?

Try this activity: Make a list of all your unmet physical and emotional needs. Now find ways to take some of the energy you spend on your teen and use it to tackle some of your own hopes and dreams. Join a support group, Bible study, or club just for you.

When you feel the exhaustion of parenting fading—and the joy returning—you'll know you're conquering your temptation to control too much. You'll be on the right track to loving just enough and, ultimately, to letting go.

Damage Control:

When Families Fracture

If God really cares, then why have all these bad things happened to me?

If God really cares, then why do I feel so alone?

If God really cares, then why is my family so messed up?

Keith jotted the questions at the top of a sheet of notebook paper—just below the title, "The Worst Year of My Life!"

The stressed-out 16-year-old had made a commitment to Christ at camp a few years back, but lately he wondered if God had given up on him. It was the perfect essay topic for Mrs. Gowler's fifth period English assignment.

Throughout the year a lot of bad things had happened to Keith: he had suffered two brain tumors that required surgery, and doctors drained fluid from his head; his dad walked out on his mom, little sister, and him; and his family had moved across the country.

And to top it off, Keith had broken his leg during a youth group ski trip. He put down his notebook and scowled at the bulky cast. "Why won't God just strike me dead and be done with me?"

His girlfriend, Cindy, who was drawing on his cast, looked up. "Don't talk that way," she said. "God isn't doing this to you. Times are hard, but He's still with you. And He'll get you through this—if you let Him."

A faint smile appeared on Keith's lips. Despite feeling lousy, he knew Cindy was right. Deep inside, he knew God hadn't left him. And when he thought about it, Christ had often revealed himself in a loving way—usually through Cindy's kind actions.

His mind flashed back to his first day of high school after moving from Los Angeles to Boston. His parents had just divorced, so he, his mom, and sister had moved to live closer to relatives. Keith was confused and bitter. He resented his family's split-up and blamed his mom. Now in a strange city, he didn't know anybody. Yet everyone at school seemed to know him.

Keith had a shaved head with a big scar on top. He also used crutches because his balance was shaky after the brain surgery. He looked as if he'd just been through a war—obviously on the losing side. And that was how everyone besides Cindy treated him.

Keith sat up on the couch and shifted the pillow under his cast. "So why do you care so much for a guy like me?" he asked.

"Because you're worth caring for," Cindy responded.

"Sure you're not just feeling sorry for a hard-luck case?"

Cindy held the marker in her hand like a dagger and raised it over Keith's chest. "Keep talking that way, and I'll put you out of your misery! If you're a hard-luck case, so am I."

Keith kissed Cindy's cheek and grinned. He knew she really cared and understood his pain.

During his first few months in Boston, Keith often skipped lunch or ate in a quiet stairwell at school. He always felt as if everyone were staring at him, so he did everything he could to stay out of sight. And his family's troubles had made him too depressed to be social. That's when he ended up meeting Cindy.

She was sitting alone in a stairwell, crying. Keith couldn't resist talking to her.

"I know you," Keith said, leaning on his crutch and tilting his head. "You're in my history class."

Cindy rubbed her eyes, and then squinted. "You're Keith, right?"

"Yeah, we both sit in the back of the room."

"Sorry, but I'm kind of a mess right now."

"What's wrong?"

Cindy wiped another tear from her cheek. "Do you have the rest of the day to listen? It's family stuff, and I'm sure I'd bore you."

"Hey, I'm an expert on family problems," Keith said carefully lowering his body beside Cindy. "In fact, I *am* a family problem."

"Well, here are my problems," Cindy said. "For starters, everybody fights all the time. And I think my parents are going to divorce."

Keith's eyes widened. Cindy definitely had his attention.

In the weeks that followed, the two formed a close friendship.

Cindy put the finishing touches on her drawings. "Voilà!" she said. "My masterpieces are finished."

Keith looked at the drawings and flashed a fake smile. "Uh, great—what are they?"

"They're cartoons of us," Cindy said, half laughing. "The dark clouds over our houses represent the problems we've had. But the two stick figures—which are supposed to be you and me—have a cross between them and the sun shining overhead. This represents our hope. Cool, huh?"

"Very cool," Keith said as he glanced into the kitchen, where his mom was preparing dinner. "You know, I've been thinking. We're survivors, aren't we?"

"No, we're conquerors," Cindy said. "God has healed you from brain tumors. And even though your parents are divorced, He has brought you and your mom and little sister closer together."

Keith locked eyes with Cindy. "He fixed your family too."

"We're far from fixed," his girlfriend said. "But at least Mom and Dad are working things out, and our church is supporting us. That's a start."

Later that night, Keith scratched out the title on his essay and scribbled the words "God Heals the Broken." Suddenly, the words flowed:

After a few years of depression and desperately wishing I could crawl into a hole and die, I met a beautiful girl named Cindy, and she helped turn on a light inside of me. When I truly began to understand who Jesus Christ was, it didn't take long for me to trust Him as my Lord, Savior, and Friend.

My family was broken and so was my heart. Even my body was weak and infected. Yet God didn't give up. He put my life in a cast, so to speak, and began the painful healing process.

All those times when I thought God didn't care, He was right there. I didn't think I had a purpose in life, but as it turns out, God was molding me for work in His kingdom.

Life hasn't been easy for my family. I've got the scars to prove it. But now I'm putting my faith on a solid-rock foundation that no one can tear down! I have a promise from God that He will never leave me or forsake me.

Broken Families

If holy matrimony is a sacred, lifetime promise men and women make before God, then why is it so casually broken in today's world? And why are so many husbands and wives viewing the marriage covenant as a legal contract that can be amended (or ended) at a later date?

Too often, "as long as we both shall live" is replaced with "as long as we both shall love." The couple agrees to share all things mutually until one or the other no longer wants to continue the relationship. At that time, they simply file the proper documents in court and are released from the contract. Property, friends, and children are divided up between the two former lovers . . . and everybody lives happily ever after, right? Wrong!

Viewing marriage as a mere contractual agreement results in misery for everyone involved—friends, family, and especially children.

During my 15 years as a youth worker, I've met so many young people whose fractured families have caused them more pain than some people endure in a whole lifetime. And in nearly every case, I've seen significantly lower self-esteem and poorer self-concepts in teens whose parents divorce than in children of intact families.

Seventeen-year-old Lorna, from Pennsylvania, is just one example. She thought her world had crashed to an end when her parents decided to split up. "I couldn't stop thinking that my parents' divorce was my fault," she says. "At times I felt so hopeless, helpless, and out of control."

Philip, a 14-year-old from Southern California, had a similar experience: "Mom and Dad argued about all kinds of stuff," he explains. "For some reason, they just couldn't get along. Their divorce hurt me deeply. It took awhile, but I eventually began to accept that none of it was my fault."

A 1998 report by the Heritage Foundation in Washington, D.C., highlighted some alarming statistics: In 1950, for every 100 children born, 12 entered a broken family. Today, for every 100 children born, 60 will enter a broken family.[1]

The percentage of children entering broken families has more than quadrupled since 1950. Each year, about 1 million children experience their parents' divorce, and 1.25 million are born out of wedlock.[2]

Hope on the Home Front

Despite the devastation caused by divorce, I've also seen God's hand at work in many broken families—bringing hope and healing in even the darkest situations.

When families fracture, I believe the goal should be for husbands and wives to reconcile and for homes to grow together again. After all, when God created marriage, He created it to be permanent—lasting for the lives of the couple. Jesus declared, "So they are no longer two, but one. Therefore what God has joined together, let man not separate" (Matt. 19:6).

But in cases where reconciliation simply won't happen, our Lord can pick up the pieces and mend the broken hearts of each person involved. The story at the beginning of this chapter is a prime example. Thanks to positive influences and the compassion of Christians in Keith's life, this young man is now a self-proclaimed "survivor turned conqueror!" He began trusting Jesus, allowing God to "put his life in a cast," and then took the first courageous steps of a long healing journey.

It was the same for Steve, a young man from Illinois. Take a look at his story: "My parents divorced when I was a freshman in high school, and it really hit me hard. I began to question a lot of stuff my parents had taught me—especially their faith. I remember thinking, 'Mom and Dad are Christians, but they still got a divorce. What's happening here?'

"My youth pastor helped me through this time and got me back on track with God. Before I had my talk with my youth pastor, I had taken my questions to the wrong people, which sent me in a lot of haywire directions."

Today, Steve has developed a better outlook on his circumstances. He now cares deeply for other hurting people, and even feels as if God has "zapped into his heart" a desire to tell others about the struggles his family has endured and how God pulled them through.

You probably know a family like Steve's or Keith's—one that has pulled apart or is on the brink of a breakup. Perhaps divorce has fractured your own family. Let's look at the needs of teenagers whose parents divorce, the stages of acceptance kids experience, and the ways God can transform divorce victims into conquerors.

Finding Sanity in a House Divided

Sarah Daniels didn't feel like eating.

This 42-year-old single parent just wanted to lock herself in her bedroom and curl up under the covers for the rest of her life.

Yet she had to think about her teenage daughter, Nicole. After all, even though Sarah had recently lost a husband, Nicole had lost a father.

"Honey, you haven't touched your spaghetti," she said to her daughter; then took a bite (to set an example). "You've got to eat or else you'll get sick."

Nicole glared at Sarah. "Too late, mother," the 16-year-old snapped. "I'm already sick; *sick* of this pathetic excuse of a family."

"Then you don't have to eat," Sarah said. "Let's talk. I'll listen. Open up and tell me what's going on inside . . ."

Nicole stood and threw her fork on the table. "Look, I don't want to talk to you or anyone. I'm finished talking." She stormed out of the kitchen.

Sarah slumped back in her chair and pushed her food away. *I don't know how to deal with this,* she thought. *It was hard enough losing my husband—now my daughter too?*

At first, Nicole had seemed strangely unemotional. Sarah remembered the day she broke the horrible news. "Your father is moving out," Sarah had told Nicole, gripping her daughter's hands, tears streaming down her face. "He wants a divorce."

Sarah could barely get the words out, yet Nicole didn't bat an eye. And in the following days, the teen avoided the topic.

Then she went through a period of anger, followed by constant bargaining: "Daddy, I'll act better if you come back," she pleaded during phone conversations with her father. "Please, please come back. You can't do this to us!"

Then Nicole became depressed and pulled away from Sarah's attempts to reach out. The weary mom was scared, confused, and desperate. Most of all, she was starting to lose her patience.

As she sat at the kitchen table, she began to think about a promise she had read in the Bible: "Fear not, for I have redeemed you; I have summoned you by name; you are mine. When you pass through the waters, I will be with you; and when you pass through the rivers, they will not sweep over you. When you walk through the fire, you will not be burned; the flames will not set you ablaze. For I am the LORD, your God, the Holy One of Israel, your Savior" (Isa. 43:1-3).

Sarah rubbed her eyes and took a deep breath. *I'm barely treading water, yet I know I've got to trust. I know I have to do everything I can to let Nicole know I really care.*

Later that evening, Sarah stood quietly by her daughter's room and poured out her heart in prayer: *Lord, I know Nicole doesn't mean to act this way. And I know that I need to be a source of strength and reach out now more than ever. Please be my source of strength. Give me the right words and actions. Most of all, don't let me lose her.*

Sarah tapped on the door. "Nicole, can I come in?"

"Whatever."

Sarah pushed open the door. "I just wanted a good-night kiss . . . and maybe a hug."

Nicole just blinked.

Sarah sat down on the edge of the bed and embraced her daughter.

Stages of Acceptance

The road ahead for Sarah and her daughter will be difficult. Yet whether Sarah realizes it or not, Nicole is on the edge of a breakthrough in the healing process. And if the teen can navigate through the depression, she will begin to accept her family's situation and regain hope for the future.

In *On Death and Dying*, psychiatrist Elisabeth Kubler-Ross

suggests six stages she feels a patient goes through when diagnosed with a terminal illness.[3] These same six stages of emotion can apply to many losses—including a teenager who is dealing with divorce.

The stages Kubler-Ross teaches can be a normal part of coping with a trauma. Here are the stages:

- ◉ **Denial:** "It didn't really happen."
- ◉ **Anger:** "It's not fair!"
- ◉ **Bargaining:** "God, if You take away this pain, I promise I'll be a better person."
- ◉ **Depression:** "I don't want to talk to anyone or do anything. Just leave me alone."
- ◉ **Acceptance:** "It happened and that's that."
- ◉ **Hope:** "It's really going to be OK."

When a young person like Nicole is suffering with grief, a parent naturally wants to fix things. But the best way you can promote healing is by letting your teen move through whatever stages of grief he or she endures. Here are six key ways you can help:

Be honest about your circumstances. Don't mask your own pain or feel you have to walk into the room with false cheerfulness. Be honest about the situation and the trauma your family is experiencing. Encourage your teen to talk, but don't force conversations.

Steer clear of wounding words. Try to not make negative comments about your former spouse. Don't force your teen to take sides.

Help your child understand it wasn't his or her fault. I have yet to meet a teen of a broken home who, at one time or another, hasn't felt to blame for the divorce.

Don't offer false hope. If reconciliation isn't in your future, help your teen understand the divorce is final.

Listen, listen, listen. As your child opens up, it's probably best not to say much. Just listen. Encourage your teen to talk. It's helpful for the grieving person to put feelings into words. At the same time, allow tears. Don't be afraid of deep emotion.

Share your heart—not your mind. If your teen asks for your opinion or advice, give it. If not, don't. But remember this: When your teen seeks advice, don't feel you have to offer the best wisdom or perfect Bible verses. A child who has lost someone through divorce has usually heard all the right answers from other caring friends and family. But the heart is where it hurts the most. So intellectual answers may not help much.

The Healing Path: A Checklist for Reaching Out

⊚ Understand that divorce is like death. It involves loss and the feelings of abandonment.

⊚ Remember that grieving people say things they don't really mean. Don't be easily offended at their words. Continue to give support even when doing so is tough.

⊚ Allow time to grieve. The grief process takes months, even years. But get help if you suspect that your teen is stuck in depression or anger.

⊚ Help your child move through his or her grief. Encourage your child to talk to your pastor, a trusted relative, or a Christian counselor.

⊚ Listen to the same story again and again, as many times as your teen needs to tell it.

⊚ Encourage your teen's friends to continue hanging out with him or her at school. If appropriate, tell them, "My teen doesn't have leprosy, just a lot of hurt."

⊚ Help your teen get on with his or her life—which means helping him or her get involved in other activities: hobbies, clubs, sports activities, drama, band.

⊚ Offer a little extra help if your young person has problems with schoolwork. As you know, when a person is grieving, it's difficult to concentrate on history and math—or even gym class.

⊚ Pray. Ask God to give you ideas to help.

⊚ Touch is especially important to someone who hurts. A loving embrace can communicate more strongly than words.

⊚ Get your teen involved in strenuous physical activities. This often alleviates emotional pressure.

Navigating Sexual Land Mines

"It used to be that teenagers would go to the movies to see adults having sex. Now adults go to the movies to see teenagers having sex" (film critic Roger Ebert [*Premiere,* 3/00]).

It seems there's no escape.

Step into a movie theater, click on the TV, or surf the Web and you can't help but wonder if morality has gone the way of the dinosaur. Tune in the radio and you're bombarded with the latest lust-driven lyrics of a current hit. All this can lead your son or daughter to believe that sexual purity is just plain weird—even for Christians!

And as if this isn't enough to keep you awake at night, consider the kinds of questions some teenagers are grappling with:

Why can't I be Christian and homosexual?
Is it a sin to just have oral sex and not intercourse?
Can I engage in group masturbation?
I've heard kids talk about bisexuality—is this wrong?

No wonder so many teenagers are confused, considering the sexual climate in which they live. For example, gay high school proms are springing up around the country. In New Orleans, organizers used a funeral home for the multischool function. Near Chicago, the First Congregational United Church of Christ in Naperville hosted a mixer for suburban students, sponsored by the Gay-Straight Alliance at Wheaton Warrenville South High.

"This is more than symbolic. This is a big step," said Nancy Mullen, executive director of DuPage Questioning Youth Center. "Every other kid gets to go to a prom as they so choose, but for [gay students] that's not an option."[1]

Despite our sex-on-credit, play-now-pay-later culture, your teenager needs to hear the truth: Not everyone is doing it.

Take the thousands who marched in the national capitals of Canada and the United States a few years ago. Proud of their virginity, and not afraid to admit it, many signed "True Love Waits" cards.

Then more than 210,000 of these cards were displayed in Washington, D.C., and Ottawa as a visual representation of teenagers all over the world who have made a pact for purity.

A moral revolution is emerging from the darkness. Is your teen a part of it?

☿ TEEN INSIGHTS ☿

Why are you taking a stand for virginity?

Alex, 18, Burlington, North Carolina: It's the right step to take if you're going to follow Christ. My virginity is a gift I want to give to my future wife. You can give it only once.

Roland, 19, Altadena, California: Sex is something made especially for marriage. To go around having it with any girl would show you don't have much consideration for God's gift.

Jeremy, 18, Houston: With premarital sex, love becomes distorted. You're not communicating love; you're actually saying, "I care more about my needs. I want to please myself."

How do you handle the pressure to have sex?

Alex: Most of us in my youth group are close friends. We encourage each other and say things like "Don't go out with this person, because you'll be too tempted to have sex."

Roland: When I get into a relationship with a girl, we make it clear that we're going out to have fun—nothing romantic. I also end dates somewhat early, because as the night progresses, thinking can become cloudy.

Jeremy: I often ask my friends tough questions, such as "How would you feel if your wife had slept around, and on your wedding night you were compared to all those other guys?" This kind of dialogue helps us stick with our commitment to stay pure.

Communicate God's Design for Sex

While God created sex as a wonderful gift to be shared by men and women in marriage, staying pure in this impure world can be a brutal struggle for many teenagers.

Take a look at what the apostle Paul wrote in 1 Thess. 4:3-5: "It is God's will that you should be sanctified: that you should avoid sexual immorality; that each of you should learn to control his own body in a way that is holy and honorable, not in passionate lust like the heathen, who do not know God."

As a parent, you have the awesome job of teaching your son or daughter biblical truth about sex. Help your teens understand why Christians must follow the Bible and believe God when He tells us to save sex for marriage. Encourage your kids to be bold enough to wait. Here are two key questions (along with some answers) to start the conversations:

QUESTION: Why does God give us sexual desires, then expect us to wait?

ANSWER: Learning sexual self-control helps a young person grow into a healthier, more fulfilled, godly person. Dr. Archibald Hart, a popular Christian psychologist, says: "The sex drive is a powerful force, and like a high-spirited stallion it needs to be brought under control if it is going to be the beautiful thing God intended it to be."[2]

BIBLE VERSE: "No temptation has seized you except what is common to man. And God is faithful; he will not let you be tempted beyond what you can bear. But when you are tempted, he will also provide a way out so that you can stand up under it" (1 Cor. 10:13).

WHAT YOU CAN DO: Dads and moms, model for your teens the healthiest sexuality you can. Teach them it's *their* responsibility (with God's help) to control their sex drives. Be honest about struggles you faced as a young person, and how you dealt with them.

QUESTION: How can premarital sex be wrong if a guy and girl love each other?

ANSWER: Some people reduce sex to simply a physical act, just another way of having fun. To them, sex = recreation. But God has a higher purpose for this wonderful gift. He wants men and women to save it for that special person who'll be their spouse for life. Unlike any other experience a married couple shares, sexual intercourse creates the deepest, most powerful bond—sort of a relational superglue. And that bond is never supposed to be separated.

BIBLE VERSE: "Flee from sexual immorality. All other sins a man commits are outside his body, but he who sins sexually sins against his own body. Do you not know that your body is a temple of the Holy Spirit, who is in you, whom you have received from God? You are not your own; you were bought at a price. Therefore honor God with your body" (1 Cor. 6:18-20).

WHAT YOU CAN DO: Parents, communicate a godly perspective on healthy sexuality. Tell your son or daughter that sex isn't just a trivial, physical act. Help your teen understand sex involves a person's body, mind, and emotions in an activity that is intended to bond a couple together for a lifetime.

Tackle the Tough Questions

We all know how dark the Internet can be. But I never fully grasped the opportunities Christians have in this cyber mission field until I received a tough question via E-mail.

While I receive hundreds of E-mails each month from teenagers, this one tugged at my heart. It was from a young man who was struggling with homosexual tendencies, and his questions were quite graphic.

I've reprinted our computer conversation in the following paragraphs. As you read it, keep in mind that his concerns represent the kinds of difficult—and even twisted—sexual issues today's youth grapple with. Likewise, my response illustrates the type of open dialogue parents and youth workers need to have with teens. Sweeping tough questions under the carpet won't do. Our kids *must* hear biblical truth—and we can't keep from sharing it.

Hey, Mike . . .

I've been having a really tough struggle with certain things lately, and I just want to get to the bottom of it all. I'd like to know the truth about male masturbation—and the issue of two or more guys masturbating together (even engaging in anal/oral intercourse with each other).

I want to know the truth on these matters and where I should stand as a Christian. What does God have to say about these things? How can I combat my feelings, desires, and fantasies?

Yours in Faith,

_____

Dear _____

I respect your courage, as well as your desire for the truth. You asked a few questions, so let's break them apart and begin with the first one.

You wanted to know if masturbation is a sin. To be honest, the Bible seems to be silent on this issue. However, most Christians who believe that masturbation is a sin quote what the Bible says about purity and lust. And I have to say, they do have a point. After all, masturbation is usually accompanied by sexual fantasies. I don't think there's anything necessarily wrong with thinking about sex, but I do think a person's sexual imagination has to be controlled. Most people who masturbate harbor fantasies that are plainly immoral. These should have no place in a Christian's life.

Why is masturbation unmentioned in the Bible? I can only conclude that it is much less significant to God than it is to most of us. A lot of young Christians—especially boys—would put masturbation as the most significant battle line in their attempt to live as Christians. God does not, apparently, consider it even worth mentioning.

So, here's my advice on this issue: Don't think of yourself as weird for having a desire to masturbate. Many other Christian guys struggle with this too. And don't harbor a bunch of guilt. Instead, talk to God about it. Honestly, God understands what you are going through. Tell Him how you feel, and ask Him for the strength to be self-controlled sexually. Ask God to help you steer clear of lust and immoral sexual fantasies.

You asked if it is a sin to masturbate with other guys or to engage in anal or oral sex with them. My answer is pretty clear: Yes, these activities are sinful and should be avoided by Christian young men.

In the Bible (1 Cor. 6:18-20, to be exact) we read: "Flee from sexual immorality. All other sins a man commits are outside his body, but he who sins sexually sins against his own body. Do you not know that your body is a temple of the Holy Spirit, who is in you, whom you have received from God? You are not your own; you were bought at a price. Therefore honor God with your body."

Several verses earlier, in 1 Cor. 6:9-10, we read: "Do not be deceived: Neither the sexually immoral nor idolaters nor adulterers nor male prostitutes nor homosexual offenders nor thieves nor the greedy nor drunkards nor slanderers nor swindlers will inherit the kingdom of God."

Rom. 1:18-32 has a lot to say on these issues. Here are some highlights: "They exchanged the truth of God for a lie . . . men also abandoned natural relations with women and were inflamed with lust for one another. Men committed indecent acts with other men, and received in themselves the due penalty for their perversion" (vv. 25, 27).

I could continue with more scriptures, but I think you get the picture.

The truth is, God made sex. He knows all about it. He even put our desires in us. But God designed sex to be experienced between a husband and a wife in marriage. Anything apart from His awesome design is apart from His will. And trust me, living apart from His will can be pretty miserable. Maybe not at first—but eventually it is.

You said that you wanted the truth about sex and that you wanted to know where you should stand as a Christian. Everything I wrote is the truth of God as I know it.

I sincerely hope you will follow God's design for sex. I realize that it can get pretty confusing—especially with the powerful sexual desires that you are dealing with. But understand this: Jesus Christ loves you and cares deeply about your struggles. (He understands them better than you do.) He will help you. As I mentioned earlier, PRAY. Tell Him everything you're feeling and ask Him for help. Jesus forgives and heals.

One more thing. Is there a trusted Christian adult you can talk to about all of this (such as your father or your pastor)? I urge you to do so. Don't carry all this alone. Get the advice of a Christian brother.

Your Friend,
Mike

LESSON FROM THE TRENCHES

How a Science Teacher Taught the "Chemistry of Romance"

by Christopher D. Zoolkoski[3]

"Is sex the only thing on a boy's mind?"

"Is *every* male a jerk?"

"I wish I could find just one guy in this world who knows how to respect a lady."

The girls in my 10th grade chemistry class at East Brooklyn Congregations High (in New York City) were mad, and a fierce argument had erupted between the sexes.

It all started when a boy in the back row insisted that it's a woman's role to "cook, clean, and have babies." A few other boys cracked some jokes about women—along with some crude remarks. That's when the ladies went ballistic (and for good reason!).

Instead of bringing the class back to the lesson on chemical compounds, I walked to the center of the room and listened. A stabbing realization ripped through my heart: *Some of my students have a warped view of sex—and could end up being destroyed by their decisions. How can I show them that purity is not only right but also the best option?*

The following day, I decided to ride the momentum. As my students walked into class, they instantly spotted the title of our lesson displayed on the overhead projector: "The Chemistry of Romance."

Love Lesson

I began by saying: "A girl might experiment with sex because, ultimately, she wants love. A guy might toy with love because he really wants sex."

Then I read some of the top 10 lines guys use on girls, such as: "If you really loved me, you'd do it," "Everybody's doing it," and "I'm so excited, I can't stop." A number of guys agreed that this is the way some boys behave toward girls. They also agreed with the statement that a girl has more to lose than a guy does when the relationship gets physical.

When Sex Is Selfish

Then we got into some real chemistry. Before class, I had secured candles to the bottoms of two glass beakers. Each beaker was labeled "Love." I placed them on opposite ends of the demonstration table.

Next to one of the beakers, I placed two others. One labeled "Sex" was partially filled with diluted sulfuric acid. The other, labeled "Selfishness," contained dry baking soda.

I lit the first candle and said, "Let's see what happens if we put some selfishness around this flame of love and then add sex to it." I spooned some baking soda around the base of the candle.

"It takes only a little bit of 'I want *my* desires to be satisfied'; just a little bit of 'I don't care how this will affect your future; let's live for the moment'—then we add some sex." As the sulfuric acid poured over the baking soda, the resulting carbon dioxide rose up and extinguished the flame. The usually rowdy class was quiet.

"Now watch what happens when we try to relight it." I struck one match after another and brought them near the smoldering wick, only to see them snuffed out.

"What could we do to rekindle this flame?" I asked.

A couple of teens responded, "You have to dump out the bad stuff."

"All right," I said. "Let's see." I took the beaker to the sink and rinsed it out. This time it took only one match to relight the flame. "If that kind of chemistry has happened to you, this shows you how to get the flame burning again. Take out selfishness—and sex."

Marriage Is the Key

Next to the second candle was a beaker with 15 percent hydrogen peroxide, also labeled "Sex," and another beaker containing manganese dioxide, labeled "Marriage."

"Around this other flame of love we'll mix a different combination." I sprinkled a bit of the manganese dioxide around the second candle. "This black powder is marriage. It also means patience and commitment and putting the other person's needs ahead of yours. When you add sex to this combination. . . ." As soon as I poured in the peroxide, the mixture began to vigorously decompose, sending pure oxygen to the flame, which burned at 10 times its original intensity, complete with bubbles, steam, and crackling noises.

About 10 seconds later, the reaction had slowed down and the flame continued to burn. The class erupted in applause—the first time they'd ever applauded one of my science lessons—and begged to see it again.

Multiple Partners = Multiple Heartache

The following week, I presented part two of "The Chemistry of Romance." I announced that the class would conduct an experiment to observe firsthand the risks of having sex with multiple partners.

For each person, I filled a test tube half-full with a mixture of water and alcohol. I announced that just one of the 25 test tubes was infected with a disease. (Earlier, I had added phenolphthalein, a clear liquid that changes color when pH levels rise above neutral, to one of the tubes.) The combination of water, alcohol, and phenolphthalein remained clear.

"The phenolphthalein could be a virus such as HIV, herpes, or hepatitis; or it could be a bacterium such as syphilis or gonorrhea," I said. "One of you is going to have this disease, but we don't know who." I let each student choose a test tube.

"Now each of you will see what happens when you have sex with someone else." I held up two test tubes. "Pour all of your solution into your partner's test tube, then your partner pours it all into your test tube, then you pour half of it back to make the amounts equal again." I demonstrated. "Now, you all do this with one other person in the room." Some students partnered with friends, while a few kids got partners they weren't happy with.

When they had completed their exchanges, I went around the room and put two drops of sodium hydroxide into each test tube. The first few test tubes remained clear. "You're healthy," I said to each of them. Then the class erupted in laughter as the next test tube turned bright pink. The student holding it was the most innocent and discreet girl in the class—the last one you'd expect to contract a sexually transmitted disease. Her partner's eyes got big, wondering if she too had been infected. As expected, her solution also turned pink, while everyone else's remained clear.

Next, I collected the test tubes, rinsed them out and repeated the exercise, infecting one test tube with phenolphthalein as before. "This time I want each of you to mix test tubes with two other people in the room."

We repeated the experiment for three and then four partners and tabulated the results on a worksheet. The data we collected was as follows: 10 percent, 25 percent, 50 percent, and 95 percent infection rates for one, two, three, and four partners.

Their homework assignment was to construct a graph of the data. I think everyone, including me, was amazed by the dramatic exponential nature of the curve and how the graphs maxed out after only four partners.

In the end, our experiment revealed that selfishness mixed with sex will always destroy a relationship. But mix the right ingredients—such as the respect and commitment found in marriage—and you've got a romantic flame that'll last a lifetime.

TUNE IN

A Pact for Purity

A few years ago, I called together a pack of teens from my church (guys who were in a discipleship group I lead), then headed to a remote spot in the Rocky Mountains.

When my group and I arrived at our destination, I shared a true story: "A friend of mine told me about a man who lost his life to AIDS a few years back. This guy had his ashes sprinkled right here. Before his death, he committed his heart to Jesus. But he also expressed some deep regrets for not being self-controlled as the Bible instructs. If he were alive today, he'd warn you to not follow the path he chose.

"Guys, you have a chance to honor God with your lives. Let's make a pact with God to live a life of purity."

Before returning home, each one of us slipped necklaces with cross pendants around our necks and vowed to remain pure. Then we spent time sharing our struggles, reading Scripture, and praying for each other.

I'm thrilled to report that years later, the guys are still wearing their crosses—and are committed to saving themselves for their future brides.

I urge you to make a pact for purity with your teens. Help them surrender their sexuality to God so He can sanctify it and give it back to them in all its glory at the proper time.

◈ Set aside uninterrupted time, find a private place, and make a **family pact for purity** with your son or daughter. Acquire a cross necklace, a ring, or a watch beforehand and present it to him or her as a symbol of purity. (Even if he or she has already done something like this at youth group, it's more powerful if he or she has this experience with Mom and Dad.)

◈ Read 2 Tim. 2:21-22.

◈ Talk openly about sexual matters and be willing to answer any question your teen may have. Even go one step further and share personal struggles you faced growing up.

◈ Communicate clearly God's design for sex.

◈ Spend some time praying for, and with, your teen.

Lost in Space: If Your Teen Rejects Christianity

Jeremy blinks as he scans the room. The 16-year-old can't believe his eyes: a basement packed with people his age drinking and openly doing every kind of drug imaginable.

"Don't be shy," says the party's host, a spooky older man wearing an all-black outfit. "Join the fun."

A friend from school smiles at Jeremy. "OK, so the guy is strange," he whispers, handing Jeremy a Budweiser, "but he throws the best parties in town."

Jeremy pops the top off the bottle and shrugs his shoulders. *It's like a wild Halloween bash,* he tells himself. *It should be good for a few laughs.*

Jeremy downs a few more beers, takes his first drag on a marijuana joint, and eventually gets so stoned he can barely stand up. A few hours later, he and the other party guests are ushered down a secret passageway that leads to a dark, musty room on one end of the basement.

Once inside, Jeremy is even more stunned. A painting of a red goat's head covers a wall, and a pentagram is drawn on the floor in the center of the room. Half the crowd—including Jeremy's friend—circles the pentagram and begins chanting strange songs. A couple of guys begin making requests to Satan.

Did that guy say . . . Satan? Jeremy asks himself, his eyes widening. *Is this for real—or is it just a weird game?*

Jeremy shrugs his shoulders again. *It's gotta be a game,* he convinces himself. *After all, the devil isn't for real.*

In the following months, he attends several more of these "wild parties." Then it happens. Jeremy awakens one night in his bed sensing a dark presence. His heart pounds hard, and he has trouble breathing. The teen realizes that something evil has taken hold of his life. Something very real . . . and very deadly. Suddenly, his fascination with the occult isn't fun anymore. What he thought would give him a few thrills he now sees as something that could destroy him.

Jeremy is scared.

◎ ⪢ ⟡ ⟡

Jeremy learned the hard way about the spiritual battle that's raging in the world. Although his name was changed to protect his identity, his story is real.

On the surface, Jeremy seemed like a model teenager. He had committed his life to Christ at an early age and was a solid member of his youth group. He was well liked at church and was often described as "a kid with his head on straight." No one knew Jeremy led a double life.

The fact is, he was bored—with church, school, and life in general. He hungered for something different from what Christianity offered. That's when Jeremy let his defenses down and turned his back on God. He met some guys at school who were into what seemed like an innocent role-playing game, so he started playing. He gradually progressed to more violent occult-oriented games . . . and eventually followed his new friends to their "wild parties," which was actually a satanic coven.

Today, Jeremy is out of the occult and back on track with God. But the young man has deep emotional scars and nightmarish memories he'll carry for the rest of his life.

While Jeremy's story may seem extreme, all teenagers are targets of the evil one. Look at these "snapshots" of ordinary teens who ended up backsliding in their faith:

Snapshot No. 1: Pain of a Fractured Faith

Kara is 14 and miserable. Her mom and dad have announced their plans to divorce, and she feels her world is crumbling around her.

This whole faith thing doesn't make sense anymore, she tells herself as she flops on her bed. Nothing makes sense. *We're a Christian family! How could they do this to me? How could God do this to me? Maybe there really isn't a God at all.*

In the following months her parents' divorce put a big crack in the faith of this Louisville, Kentucky, teen. Her non-Christian friends are the only ones who seem to make sense to her. Kara gradually rejects church—as well as everyone from youth group.

"Why should I follow a God who lets you down," she tells her parents.

Snapshot No. 2: Rebel Without a Cause

Skating isn't easy in a place like Pamlico Beach, North Carolina. The biggest problem? There aren't many paved roads.

But that doesn't stop 14-year-old Lenny. The young man is often outside his home, dragging plywood into his front yard so he'll have a smooth surface to practice on.

Lenny is facing far more problems than finding a place to skate. Vandalism, robbery, and constant brushes with the law have been a part of Lenny's youth, even before his 10th birthday.

"I'm convinced that I'm Satan's tool in giving my family a hard time," Lenny tells concerned people who reach out to his family.

Then, with a smirk, he adds: "I almost died at birth, and that's where it began. Everyone in the neighborhood thinks I'm crazy. People don't want their kids near me. Nobody can handle me—not my parents, not my probation officer . . . no one. And I'm OK with that."

Although he is in a Christian home, Lenny no longer wants to have anything to do with faith. He seems to be bent on self-destruction, and his parents are clueless about what to do.

Then one day Lenny convinces himself that "freedom" is on the other side of the country—far away from his parents. He joins a group of older guys for a road trip to California.

Snapshot No. 3: Getting Back on Track

"Stop living a lie, Troy."

"Your life's out of control."

"Want to do something worthwhile with yourself? Start by giving everything to Jesus."

The words echo through Troy's head, leaving a sickening pain in the pit of his stomach. *My parents are right,* the 15-year-old tells himself. My life is falling apart.

The Southern Californian knows his world has already slipped over the edge—and that he is tumbling into a deadly pit of drugs, street violence, and "nowhere friendships" that have gotten him kicked out of school and in trouble with the law.

Troy squeezes shut his eyes and begins to pray. "Lord, I don't know how I went from being a good Christian kid to turning my back on You," he says out loud, his heart pounding. "But I've got to make a change. I was stupid to give into drugs, and I was crazy to listen to my friends. But now I'm giving my life to You."

Troy opens his eyes and feels the peace of God. Suddenly, the pain in his stomach goes away.

For once in my life, I've done something right, he tells himself.

❂   ⸙   ℘   ℘

Satan is working overtime to lure our youth into a hostile position toward God, and he uses every kind of distraction imaginable—boredom, selfish desires, inferiority, drug abuse, doubt, fear, materialism, and more. The list could fill a book.

Satan's biggest ally is your young person's flesh, which is the human, physical dimension of your teen's life that instinctively wants to live independently from God. Even though your child now has a new nature in Christ, the sinful world still tempts him or her to return to those old ways of thinking and living. (See Rom. 8:5-8 and Eph. 2:3.)

So, as a parent, what can you do? How can your teen survive? The answer is basic, but vital—and one repeated throughout this book: You need to steer your teen to a personal, active relationship with Jesus Christ. The Lord is your family's ultimate ally—your ultimate defender.

Get Your Teen Grounded

❂ **Know the enemy's tactics.** Satan knows just which buttons to push to tempt you away from depending on Christ. He has watched your behavior over the years and knows where you are weak. That's where he attacks. Teach your teen this vital truth.

◉ **Choose your weapons.** We can show our teens that while they can't outsmart or outmuscle the flesh or the devil alone, they can find victory over struggles against sin. The Lord has armed every Christian with spiritual weapons packed full of "divine power": (1) The sword of the spirit—the Holy Bible—and (2) prayer. Col. 3:16 tells Christians to let "the word of Christ dwell in you richly," and Phil. 4:7 promises that "the peace of God . . . will guard your hearts and your minds in Christ Jesus."

◉ **Follow your defender.** Merely hanging out at church and "doing your Christian duty" doesn't cut it. Youth need to know Jesus personally. He is the greatest conqueror ever, and with His guidance, teens can have victory over the devil.

◉ **Help them understand that God always cares.** Too many teens feel God has turned His back on them when hard times hit. Teach your son or daughter that, no matter how hard life gets, the Lord won't give them more than they can handle. Say: "You may feel as if you're about to break, but that's when the Lord steps in to restore you." For a great example from the Bible, turn to Job and read your teen the story about what this man of faith went through—and how God helped him.

◉ **Teach them to look to the Bible for answers.** David was called a man after God's own heart. Yet he's a guy who did some pretty bad stuff, like adultery. Sometimes David was on top of the world. But at other times, he was a complete mess. Tell your teen, "You're not any less of a Christian when you feel frustrated in your walk with Christ or when your life is full of troubles. At times just about every believer hits bottom. And during those times, we need to stand strong—not retreat from what we believe. While we don't always sense it, God actually draws closer to us when we face trials, if we let Him."

How to Raise a Cult-Free Kid

How many sheep will the shepherds lose? Author and cult expert Jim Foster says scores of young people join around 3,000 cults each year, often on college campuses. "Many of these youth are Christians who lack maturity," Jim explains. "Some of these kids have not been taught to identify and deal with cult recruiters."

In 1984, Jim's son, Kraig, was lost to a roving "Christian" cult on his California campus called The Brethren.

"Kraig's 'church' is the epitome of a Bible-based cult," Jim says. "It's nomadic. Members separate from the world (including all family and friends) and yield to the absolute control of the elder. 'Witnessing' is essentially recruiting."

Jim admits that retrieving someone from a cult is difficult. The victim often adopts the group's beliefs and experiences a breakdown in rational thought. Trying to talk them out of their new beliefs is usually impossible. Unless members see someone as a potential recruit, they are reluctant to discuss their beliefs. They fear outsiders and are taught that leaving the group will cost them their salvation.

"An ounce of prevention is worth a hundred-weight of cure," Jim says. "My 16 years of experience in the world of cults has revealed, time after time, how tough it is to prepare young people to identify and walk away from cult recruiters. If you've never talked with a cult member, seek out a Mormon Missionary or a Jehovah's Witness and challenge their beliefs. It will give you some idea of how hard it is for young Christians to fend off spiritual predators."

Since thousands of cults exist, it's impossible to educate young people about each one. While Jim's son, Kraig, wears distinctive clothing, other cult members aren't as easy to identify. Many cultists dress as we do, making it impossible to single them out. And while some cults on campus are extremely open, they often use a palatable doctrine as bait until the hook is set and it's too late for their catch to realize they're being reeled in.

Jim urges you to try these effective means of preparing students to identify and fend off cult recruiters:

⊚ **Convince your teen that he or she is no match for a well-trained cultist.** Jim says recruiters know the Bible better and can express their beliefs more forcefully than 90 percent of all Christians. Also, these people often lie and twist Scripture.

⊚ **Get the facts.** If your teen is approached by a stranger (or a "friend of a friend") who wants to talk about Jesus or even someone who wants to invite him or her to a Bible study, issue an invitation of your own. Have your teen ask the stranger to visit with you or your pastor first. If the stranger attempts to put off such a meeting or says, "It's your decision, not someone else's," your teen should walk away.

Size up the situation. If such a stranger uses Christ's words of Scripture to intimidate, produce guilt, or attack mainline denominations, a young person should end the conversation. They are probably being sized up by a recruiter.

◎ ⸙ ⸎ ⸏

"I cannot emphasize strongly enough that Christians who are immature in the Word (despite having studied it for years) are no match for most cult recruiters," Jim says. "The adolescent who nobly tries to confront such ideologies often ends up being the one enlisted.

"My son Kraig left six pages of notes and questions he had written as the recruiter was working on him," Jim adds. "In different colored ink he scribbled the answers, derived either independently or with the cultist's help. He even wrote down the question, 'Is this group a cult?' His response: 'No.'"

Jim explains that it took the recruiter five days to ensnare his son's heart and mind. Kraig left his family on April 7, 1984. His mother has seen him once and his father has seen him twice in the past several years.

Jim's advice: "Shepherds, prepare your sheep."

LESSON FROM THE TRENCHES
A Young Man's Journey Back to God

K. P. Westmoreland of Oklahoma City nearly ended his life. But a radical encounter with God put him on an eternal track.

K. P. is amazed at how God accomplishes His work through the talents of obedient Christians . . . even the crazy antics of a modern-day basketball player.

"The key word is OBEDIENT, not perfect," K. P. says. "But it took years for me to learn this truth. As a young man, I ended up wandering in the wrong direction. But God eventually got me back on the right course."

While K. P. was raised in a Christian home, he escaped into basketball at age 12 when his parents announced: "We're getting a divorce."

"It tore me apart," K. P. says. "I couldn't understand how this could happen to my Christian family. Basketball became my hope—even though it was a false hope.

"I thought that the better I was at the sport, the better my life would be. I thought I could get a college scholarship, end up playing with the pros and making big bucks, and all of my problems would be solved. I was wrong."

Meanwhile, his church continued to reach out to him and his family. The first verse K. P. ever read was 1 Tim. 4:12: "Don't let anyone look down on you because you are young, but set an example for the believers in speech, in life, in love, in faith and in purity."

"I attended a youth retreat and asked Jesus into my heart," K. P. says. "But within hours, I was the same old K. P. It was just an emotional experience, and I didn't get into the Bible or pray."

K. P. made a genuine commitment to Jesus during his sophomore year of college, a time he describes as "wild and self-destructive."

"At parties, I never drank just one beer," K. P. says. "I drank to the extreme. It was the same with drugs. I was very angry inside—maybe because of my parents' divorce. Still, I don't blame them. I made my own stupid choices."

Late one night, as he sat alone in his apartment and snorted line after line of cocaine, he lashed out at God. "Kill me," he screamed. "Let me die of an overdose. I don't want to live anymore. Please, please let me die."

K. P. curled up in a tiny ball on the floor and fell asleep. When he awoke later, he looked at himself in a mirror and gasped.

"I didn't recognize the face staring back at me," he says. "I looked dark and distorted.

"I was disgusted with my life. My girlfriend and I had gone too far and destroyed an innocent baby because of our sin. I was strung out on drugs and hated everyone who tried to get close to me. I knew I had to change."

The weary young athlete dropped to his knees and began to cry. "Lord, You're going to have to take away my desire to self-destruct. You'll have to change me—because I can't do it alone."

Overnight, his desire for drugs was wiped away, and K. P. took his first real steps in the right direction. "A year later, I hit my knees at my mom's house," he says. "This time, I asked Jesus to be not just my Savior, but to be the Lord of my life."

God took hold of K. P.'s life and set him on a course he never imagined he'd follow.

Today, he operates his own basketball ministry, performing in public schools and prisons. "I've recruited guys I'd played with in high school and college, and we play pickup basketball games against prison teams.

"The Lord has opened doors, and I'm just trying to be faithful," K. P. adds. "And that's what being a Christian is all about. I just can't say it enough: You don't have to be perfect to make an impact—just obedient. If God can use a past drug abuser like me, I know He can definitely use anyone!"

CONCLUSION
Lessons from the Edge

Before we end our journey through the alien world of teenagers, let's return to the desert Southwest and the rock climbing expedition we saw at the beginning of this book.

The teen girl in my opening story had good reason to celebrate. On her first climb up a steep rock face, she faced her fears, pressed ahead, and successfully joined her parents at the top of the canyon.

I, too, faced the difficult challenge of scaling that same sandstone wall near Moab, Utah. (It's located in a section of the desert called Wall Street!) I stared in disbelief at my destination—a ledge 40 feet above me. I felt completely unprepared for the task at hand. *This is insane!* I told myself. *I can't climb this! The wall seems too flat and way too steep.*

Sensing my doubt, our professional guide patted me on the back. "You're ready—I promise," he said with a smile. "We've covered the basics together. Now think through each step and have faith. The rope will protect you."

Just as I mustered up the tiniest ounce of courage, reality hit.

Todd, an 18-year-old who was climbing ahead of me on a more difficult part of the wall, suddenly lost his grip and began to swing helplessly across the rock. He scraped up his arms and legs. My legs weakened as I watched. But then I remembered the guide's advice: "The rope will protect you."

It really works! I told myself. *Todd won't fall!*

The strong nylon line attached to Todd's safety harness literally saved his life. In fact, Todd eventually regained control—as well as his confidence—and even made it to the ledge near the top of the canyon wall!

"I was learning fairly quickly, then I slipped," he told me later. "My head was pounding, and I felt as if I had nothing to hold on to. I guess I tried too steep of a climb for the first time. My lesson: Listen to my instructor, plan ahead, and don't tackle too much, too soon."

116   ◎ **HOW TO SPEAK ALIEN**

Powerful lessons for rock climbing—and life!

◎ ⚘ ⚲ ☙

The fact that you're reading this book means you care enough to help your teen through the "canyon of adolescence." You want a trusting relationship with your son or daughter—the kind I described earlier.

I assure you, the terrain ahead will be difficult at times, but not impossible to navigate. Let me end with a few simple but life-changing lessons I learned during my rock climbing adventure.

Secure Your Teen to God's Word

When it comes to spiritual matters, how does your child measure? Is he or she secured to a vibrant, growing relationship with Jesus Christ? Or is your son or daughter climbing danger-ously through adolescence kamikaze style—solo (relying on his or her own strength) and without the proper gear (a worldview grounded in the Bible)?

As I mentioned earlier, parenting teenagers involves guiding them up a steep rock face known as adolescence. And the key to their success depends upon their training from you.

Follow the advice of Deut. 6:5-7: "Love the LORD your God with all your heart and with all your soul and with all your strength. These commandments that I give you today are to be upon your hearts. Impress them on your children. Talk about them when you sit at home and when you walk along the road, when you lie down and when you get up."

Nurture Growth from Failure

When the going gets rough for your teen, trust the safety harness. "Be still, and know that I am God" (Ps. 46:10).

But what about those times when your child blatantly re-jects your authority—or even your faith? Let's look at the para-ble of the lost son (Luke 15:11-32).

In this passage a caring dad experiences the battle of wills with his headstrong son . . . and watches as he slides helplessly down the rock face of youth. "Dad, I'm leaving home, and you can't stop me."

How would you react in this type of situation? "Go ahead and leave, but don't think you can come crawling back. You'll find no sympathy here!"

The Bible gives us a better course of action. As we get to the end of the story in Luke 15, we quickly discover a profound truth—God's ways are not our ways. From a spiritual standpoint, we are all as rebellious as the prodigal son. And each time we blow it, we expect—and feel we deserve—rejection, along with the "I told you you'd mess it up" speeches. Yet we get just the opposite from God. Our loving Father always waits and welcomes us home with open arms. When we seek Jesus Christ and repent, He forgives.

Does this mean we excuse what our kids have done wrong? Of course not. Prov. 12:1 rather bluntly says: "Whoever loves discipline loves knowledge, but he who hates correction is stupid." The key is balanced, godly discipline. This means . . .

- ◉ *acting on the promptings of the Holy Spirit*
- ◉ *not reacting out of anger*
- ◉ *never saying the words "Don't come back!"*

There is an appropriate time and place for tough love—the kind of approach needed when a child is so out of control, it's the only way to get him or her back on course. Yet many parents are rigid with discipline when it is not really called for.

Instead, be the kind of parent who disciplines with love and who seeks to nurture growth from failure.

Pray for Protection

It was hard watching Todd slide down the rock face. Adrenaline pulsed through every vein in my body. (I can only imagine how Todd felt.) But as this young man struggled to regain control and get back on course, he wasn't alone. Several of us began to pray for him:

"Lord, protect Todd."

"Father, give him strength right now."

"Jesus, help him find a way out of this jam."

"O God in heaven, enable Todd to make it to the top of the ledge."

Later, when he had gotten through the ordeal, I overheard a conversation Todd had with another teen: "I was scared, but I know the prayers of others really helped. It's really cool knowing that the adults on this trip care enough to pray for me."

Prayer is powerful. God works through our prayers and changes lives. He will do the same for your teenager. But do you regularly pray for your son or daughter? Do you pray with him or her?

I challenge you to make prayer a priority in your home. As we close, I'm offering you a prayer of hope, faith, and healing for your family. It's my hope that you pray this, or something like it, every day.

Prayer of Hope, Faith, Healing

O Lord God, I ask that You make our home a place of love and peace and light . . .

> Where security is found.
> Where trust is taught.
> Where forgiveness is modeled.
> Where faith is lived.

O Lord God, draw my teenager close to You. Protect him in Your arms and let him sense Your power today—the holy, eternal power that can set him free.

> Free from the bondage of sin.
> Free to live life as a gift of grace.
> Free to dream, free to take risks, free to fail.
> Free to live in faith and in hope and in love.

O Lord God, let Your truth be the anchor of my family. Restore, repair, renew . . . and heal our lives.

> Heal brokenness.
> Heal rejection.
> Heal hostility.
> Heal fear.

O Lord God, how we need Your hope. I commit my family to You. Let us honor You in our home. Amen.

ENDNOTES

Chapter 1. Mysteries of the Teen Zone

1. Larry Dumont, *Surviving Adolescence* (New York: Villard Books, 1991), 28.

2. George Barna, "Third Millennium Teens," a survey conducted January 2000 by the Barna Research Group, Ltd., Ventura, Calif.

3. Bruce Narramore, *Adolescence Is Not an Illness* (New Jersey: Fleming H. Revell, 1980), 61.

4. David Elkind, *All Grown Up and No Place to Go* (Reading, Mass.: Addison-Wesley Publishing Co., 1984), 6-8.

5. Lissa Halls Johnson, "Living for the Moment." Used by permission of the author.

Chapter 2. Making Contact: Getting Through to Your Teen

1. Paul W. Swets, *The Art of Talking with Your Teenager* (Holbrook, Mass.: Adams Publishing, 1995), 16.

2. Robert S. McGee, *The Search for Significance* (Houston: Rapha Publishing, 1990), 29.

3. Thomas Gordon, *Parental Effectiveness Training (P.E.T.) in Action: The No-Lose Way to Raise Happier, More Responsible, More Cooperative Children* (New York: Bantam Books, 1988), 117.

4. Dumont, *Surviving Adolescence,* 218.

5. Chuck Swindoll, *Growing Wise in Family Life* (Sisters, Oreg.: Multnomah Publishers, 1988), 152.

Chapter 3. Invade Your Teens' Worlds (Without Invading Their Space)

1. Bill Sanders, *Almost Everything Teens Want Parents to Know but Are Afraid to Tell Them* (Wheaton, Ill.: Tyndale House Publishers, 1994), 64.

2. Cheryl Sloan Wray, "How You Can Be a Role Model." Used by permission of the author.

Chapter 4. Parent and Teen Hot Spots

1. Gary Chapman, "Listening to Teenage Anger," first appeared in *Living with Teenagers,* June 1995, pp. 24-26, and is used with the author's permission.

Chapter 6. Is Dad Missing in Action?

1. Robert L. Maginnis, statement from a speech delivered to the World Congress of Families, titled "Challenges to Children's Well-Being," November 15, 1999, Geneva, Switzerland.

2. "Statistical Abstract of the United States: 1998" (Washington, D.C.: U.S. Department of Commerce, Bureau of the Census, 1998), 69.

3. M. Anne Hill and June O'Neill, *Underclass Behaviors in the United States:*

Measurement and Analysis of Determinants (New York: City University of New York, 1993).

4. "The Impact of Father Absence and Family Breakdown on Children's Educational Attainment," Family Research Council, *InFocus,* February 1993.

5. David Blankenhorn, *Fatherless America* (New York: Basic Books, 1995), 46.

6. U.S. Department of Health and Human Services, National Center for Health Statistics, Survey on Child Health, Washington, D.C.: U.S. Government Printing Office, 1993.

7. "Our Father's Day Poll Results," ABC News, June 22, 1998.

8. Donald M. Joy, *Becoming a Man* (Ventura, Calif.: Regal Books, 1990), 32.

9. Ibid.

Chapter 7. The Wonderful World of Mom

1. Dr. James Dobson, *Solid Answers* (Wheaton, Ill.: Tyndale House Publishers, 1997), 78.

2. Richard Carlson, *Don't Sweat the Small Stuff* (New York: Hyperion, 1998), 1.

Chapter 8. Damage Control: When Families Fracture

1. Patrick F. Fagan, "The Breakdown of the Family," *Issues '98: The Candidate's Briefing Book* (Washington, D.C.: Heritage Foundation, 1998), 171.

2. Ibid.

3. Elisabeth Kubler-Ross, *On Death and Dying* (New York: Macmillan Publishing Co., 1969).

Chapter 9. Navigating Sexual Land Mines

1. Tracy Dell'Angela, "The Freedom to Be Themselves," *Chicago Tribune,* May 16, 2000.

2. Dr. Archibald Hart, *The Sexual Man* (Dallas: Word Publishing, 1994), n.p.

3. Christopher D. Zoolkoski, "The Chemistry of Romance." Used by permission of the author.

Chapter 10. Lost in Space: If Your Teen Rejects Christianity

1. Jim Foster, "How to Raise a Cult-Free Kid," first appeared in Focus on the Family's *Plugged In* magazine, June 2000, p. 9, and is used by permission of the author.